FROM CHAINS TO WINGS

A Poetry Revolution for Healing

Joy Stephenson-Laws, JD

FROM CHAINS TO WINGS

A Poetry Revolution for Healing

ABOUT THIS BOOK

This book weaves together my personal journey with patterns I've observed over decades. At its heart is the story of my son and me learning to recognize our inherited anxiety patterns.

To protect privacy while illuminating universal experiences: - My son (called "Kyle" here) is real. His core story—the hypervigilance, the panic attacks, our parallel healing journeys—is true. Some of Kyle's experiences have been expanded to include similar patterns I've seen in others, making his story both personal and representative.

Conversations are reconstructed from memory and journals, compressed for clarity. - All names except mine have been changed.

I am not a therapist or medical professional. I'm a healthcare attorney who spent forty years analyzing medical records, then became a certified holistic coach after watching my son struggle with patterns I'd passed down. What I share comes from our lived experience, research, and observation—not clinical training.

The information in this book is not medical or psychological treatment. Please consult qualified healthcare providers for mental health concerns. If in crisis, call 988 (Suicide & Crisis Lifeline).

Cover design: Brittany Dixon

Cover and interior artwork: Jay Johansen

ISBN (Paperback): 979-8-9939740-1-9

ISBN (Hardcover): 979-8-9939740-0-2

First Edition: 2025
Printed in the United States of America 10 9 8 7 6 5 4 3 2 1

For more information, visit:
phlabs.org

AUTHOR'S NOTE

My son has PTSD. Watching him navigate inherited anxiety patterns while confronting my own has been the hardest and most educational experience of my life. His story forms the foundation of this book.

To protect privacy and illustrate how universal these patterns are, I've done the following:

- Changed all names except mine and Kyle's
- Reconstructed conversations from memory
- Compressed timelines for clarity
- Combined some of his experiences with similar stories from my coaching practice

When you read about "Kyle," you're reading about my real son, but some stories include elements from others with similar struggles. I made this choice to show how common these patterns are while maintaining privacy.

I am not a therapist. I'm a healthcare attorney who became a certified holistic coach after traditional approaches weren't helping my family. I spent forty years analyzing medical records and evaluating research claims. This trained me to distinguish evidence from speculation, but it doesn't make me a mental health professional.

What I offer here comes from:

- Our family's lived experience
- Patterns observed in my coaching practice
- Research I've evaluated as an informed layperson
- Approaches we tried on ourselves

This is not medical or psychological treatment. For mental health concerns, work with qualified professionals. If you're in crisis, call 988 (Suicide & Crisis Lifeline) or text HOME to 741741 (Crisis Text Line).

Content warning: This book discusses childhood trauma, panic, dissociation, and family dysfunction. Take breaks as needed. Skip what doesn't serve you.

Your healing will look different from ours. *Take what helps. Leave the rest.*

For Kyle,

who had the courage to let his story help others,

even when the healing wasn't complete.

And for everyone who checks the locks at 3 AM,

leaves their body when things get intense, or

wonders if they're broken:

You're not.

We're all still practicing.

TABLE OF CONTENTS

FROM CHAINS TO WINGS

A Poetry Revolution for Healing

* * *

You know that thing where you check the locks five times, hate yourself for it, check them once more anyway, then lie awake wondering what's wrong with you?

Nothing's wrong with you.

Your body is doing exactly what it learned to do to keep you safe. Maybe it learned this when you were five, or fifteen, or last year when everything fell apart. The checking, the scanning, the leaving your body when things get intense—these aren't character flaws. They're survival strategies that worked once.

The problem is they're still running.

I'm Joy, and I check locks too. Also scan every room for exits, say yes when I mean no, and learned anxious patterns from a mother who learned them from her mother who had her own good reasons for staying vigilant.

For forty years as a healthcare attorney analyzing medical records and evaluating research claims, I understood trauma intellectually. Could explain the neuroscience, cite the studies. None of that knowledge stopped me from checking those locks. Or watching my son Kyle (whose story I sometimes expand with similar patterns I've seen in others) develop the same patterns.

What finally helped wasn't more analysis. It was developing awareness—learning to notice "Oh, I'm doing that checking thing again." Not fixing it. Just seeing it clearly. That seeing creates a tiny space where choice becomes possible.

The title captures this transformation: from feeling chained to patterns, to finding freedom through awareness. Not freedom from patterns—they still arise. But freedom to see them, understand them, sometimes choose differently.

Through three parts, you'll develop awareness that makes change possible:

Part One: Recognizing Your Patterns

Four chapters on developing awareness of what your nervous system does and why—seeing patterns as intelligence, not dysfunction

Part Two: Learning to Move

Awareness of your current state so you can choose practices that actually match your nervous system's needs

Part Three: Relationships as Practice

Awareness of how patterns emerge between nervous systems—maintaining consciousness when triggered

Each chapter opens with a poem. As an attorney trained in logic and overthinking, I've found poetry offers something different—it makes me feel rather than analyze. Simple poetic images often create instant recognition where lengthy explanations fail.

This isn't a quick-fix manual. It's for those ready to develop awareness as the foundation for lasting change. If you're in crisis, please call 988 (Suicide & Crisis Lifeline) or text HOME to 741741.

The journey from chains to wings begins with simply noticing what is.

Ready?

* * *

Next: Part One — Recognizing Your Patterns
Understanding what your nervous system does and why

Rather than polishing the mirror, take care of the image it reflects – we change the reflection by changing ourselves.

Collaboration with Joy Laws & Artist Jay Johansen

PART ONE

RECOGNIZING YOUR PATTERNS

Understanding what your nervous system does and why

PART ONE: RECOGNIZING YOUR PATTERNS

You're either lost in a pattern or aware of it happening. There's no in-between.

When you're lost in checking locks, you ARE the checking. When anxiety floods, you ARE the anxiety. No separation exists between you and the experience. But sometimes—mid-check, mid-panic—you catch yourself: "I'm doing that thing again."

That catch changes everything.

Not because the pattern stops. It doesn't. You still check the lock. The anxiety still floods. But now 1% of you observes while 99% experiences. That 1% is where choice lives.

Four chapters develop this observer capacity:

Chapter 1: You're Not Broken

Learn to distinguish having anxiety from being consumed by it. The difference between "I'm anxious" and "I notice anxiety" creates space for choice.

Chapter 2: Your Inner Protector

Recognize when pulling back from good things might be wisdom, not self-sabotage. Sometimes your body knows what your mind doesn't.

Chapter 3: When Your Body Speaks

Notice where tension lives—jaw, shoulders, stomach. Physical symptoms often connect to emotional patterns, though the connections vary by person.

Chapter 4: Finding One Safe Place

When everything feels activated, locate one neutral spot—an earlobe, a knee. This becomes your anchor.

Each chapter asks you to notice, not fix. You'll want strategies immediately. Part Two provides them. But you can't change what you can't see clearly.

This frustrates some readers. "I know my patterns," they say. But knowing about patterns and catching them mid-action are different skills. One is thinking. The other is recognizing yourself in real-time.

Try this: Notice whether you're absorbed in reading or aware that you're reading. Can you do both? That split attention—that's your observer developing.

* * *

My patterns aren't problems to fix.

They're protective strategies that once helped.

In Part One, I'm just noticing:

What patterns do I have?

When do they show up?

What might they be protecting?

That observation—that tiny space of awareness—

changes everything.

Not because it stops the patterns,

but because it reminds you:

You are more than your protective strategies.

Awareness comes first.

Understanding follows.

Change, if needed, comes later.

For now, I just notice.

* * *

Next: Chapter 1 — You're Not Broken

Your body is doing what it learned to do

CHAPTER 1

You're Not Broken

Your body is doing what it learned to do

* * *

> **Today's Focus**
>
> *Simply notice your protective patterns. They developed for a reason.*

Your First Awareness Practice

Right now, notice your body. Are your shoulders tight? Is your jaw clenched? Are you holding your breath? Where do you feel tension?

Don't try to relax. Just notice.

That noticing—that's the entire practice we'll build on.

That noticing you just did? I call it observer capacity. Some people call it the witness. Others call it awareness. Whatever name you use, it's the part of you that can step back and see what's happening without being completely caught up in it. Now let's understand what you're observing—how these patterns formed and why they persist.

THE BODY LEARNS FIRST

Some patterns drift in family air—
before fear has words,
the body already knows
to flinch when voices rise.

Shoulders climb.
Armor to the ears.
Storms that ended long ago
still rumble inside the chest.

Others we invent—
the lock checked again. Again.
Because once—
the door was open.

Some of us left early.
Burned gardens before frost.
Broke good things while they were good.

These aren't flaws.
They're stitches of survival,
shells we grew overnight.

And still—
we stand here breathing,
proof that the body
found a way through.

I know because I checked my locks three times this morning. I knew they were locked after the first check—I watched myself turn the deadbolt, tested the handle. But my body insisted: check again. And again. Each time feeling both ridiculous and compelled.

Your body isn't broken. It's doing exactly what it learned to do to keep you safe. The problem is it's still running protection protocols from dangers that passed years—sometimes decades—ago.

My body learned vigilance from my mother, who learned it from necessity after my father died when I was four. One woman and a small child alone on an isolated farm—she'd step onto the porch each night and throw firecrackers into the darkness. The crack echoing across the fields sounded like warning shots, telling anyone listening we were armed and awake. I absorbed that vigilance without words. Every night, watching my mother perform her safety ritual—checking windows, loading the firecrackers, listening for sounds that didn't belong—I learned that survival meant never fully trusting that you're safe. You check, then check again. You perform safety, then perform it once more to be sure.

She had her firecrackers and her route through the house. I have my locks and my own ritual: front door, back door, windows, front door again. The tools changed but the pattern remained: safety isn't a state you achieve but something you must constantly verify. Now, forty years later, my body still runs her program—just with different props.

The Core Truth:
You Have Patterns, You Aren't Them

Here's what took me decades to understand: I am not anxious. I have anxiety sometimes. The difference changes everything. When you say "I am anxious," you're completely identified with the pattern. When you say "I have anxiety," you acknowledge it as something you experience, not something you are. There's you, and there's the pattern that sometimes runs. That separation—however tiny—is where choice begins.

This isn't minimizing your experience. For some people, anxiety is so persistent it feels like identity. That's valid. But studies on metacognitive awareness suggest that when we can observe our patterns—even while they're running—something may shift in how the brain processes the experience. While research is ongoing, many people report that simply noticing their patterns—even without stopping them—changes their relationship to those patterns. You're still anxious, but not only anxious. There's a part watching the anxiety happen.

Think of it this way: When you're completely absorbed in anxiety, you're in the movie. When you can observe "I'm having anxiety," you're suddenly aware you're watching a movie—still affected by it, still feeling it, but not exclusively defined by it.

* * *

How These Patterns Form

Last month my GPS rerouted me through unfamiliar streets at night. Within seconds, my hands gripped the wheel, breath shallow, eyes jumping to mirrors. Nothing happened. No one followed. But my body was certain: danger.

Your nervous system develops these responses through multiple pathways:

- **Implicit learning before memory:** Children's nervous systems shape themselves through thousands of daily interactions with caregivers. If your parent startled at loud noises, your body learned—without words—that sudden sounds meant danger. If they checked locks repeatedly, your body absorbed that vigilance was necessary for safety.

- **Direct experience:** Sometimes you develop patterns from your own experiences. A break-in creates checking rituals. A car accident makes you hypervigilant while driving. Your body remembers threats and stays ready.

- **Cultural and family transmission:** Beyond individual trauma, we inherit cultural patterns of vigilance. Families who survived persecution carry heightened alertness. Communities that faced violence maintain protective behaviors generations later. These aren't pathologies— they're inherited wisdom that may no longer apply.

Illustration

Understanding patterns intellectually is one thing. Seeing them reflected back by someone who loves you—that's when the blind spots become visible. This conversation with Kyle shows how recognition often comes through another's eyes:

A Conversation About Inherited Patterns

My son Kyle is thirty-one now. We've had this conversation more than once:

Kyle: "Mom, why do you have so many dogs?"

Me: "Five German Shepherds? They make me feel safe."

Kyle: "I get it. I do the same thing, just differently. Remember when my GPS routed us through that unfamiliar neighborhood?"

Me: "I was practically hyperventilating. And I've never been robbed. Never been attacked. But my body acted like I was in actual danger."

Kyle: "That's what I mean. We both do it."

Me: "I've been researching this. It's called inherited hypervigilance. Our nervous systems learn patterns from watching our parents, even before we can form memories."

Kyle: "The firecrackers. I know."

Me: "Do you know why she did it?"

Kyle: "To scare animals?"

Me: "To sound like gunshots. After Dad died, it was just her and me—a fifty-year-old woman and a four-year-old child alone on an isolated farm. She wanted anyone within earshot to think we had guns and weren't afraid to use them."

Kyle: "Jesus. You were four?"

Me: "Four. Learning that safety meant constant vigilance and performing strength we didn't have. The research shows kids' nervous systems literally shape themselves around their caregivers' stress patterns."

Kyle: "So when I watch you check locks…"

Me: "You're learning the same thing I learned watching her with those firecrackers. Different method, same message: stay ready."

Me: "But here's what I've discovered—if we can notice the pattern while it's happening, we create a tiny gap between trigger and response. That gap is where choice lives."

Kyle: "You mean stop checking locks?"

Me: "No, that's forcing change. I mean notice yourself checking. 'Oh, there I go, checking again.' Studies on metacognitive awareness suggest that observing a pattern without judgment may influence how the brain processes it. While research is ongoing, many people

14

report that simply noticing their patterns—even without stopping them—changes their relationship to those patterns."

Kyle: "So just… watch myself do it?"

Me: "Exactly. I still check, but now I notice myself doing it. Sometimes I even laugh—'Hello, old pattern.' Doesn't stop it, but something's different."

Kyle intuited what neuroscience confirms: these aren't just habits we can drop. They're encoded in our nervous systems through processes that begin before conscious memory.

Understanding Your Body's Alarm System

Your body's threat detection involves multiple brain regions working together. When something triggers this system—real danger or just reminders of past danger—your body responds before conscious thought engages.

Here's what research has established:

- **Your nervous system can't distinguish between actual threats and reminders of past threats.** The same physiological cascade happens whether facing real danger or something that resembles old danger. This isn't a malfunction—it's how we survived as a species. Better to overreact to a stick that looks like a snake than under-react to an actual snake.

- **The response happens faster than thought.** By the time your conscious mind recognizes "that's just a shadow," your body has already flooded with stress hormones, tensed muscles and quickened breath. The body decides first, then informs the mind.

- **Patterns strengthen through repetition.** Each time you check the locks and feel momentarily safer, your brain reinforces the connection: checking = safety. The pattern becomes more automatic and more compelling.

- **Change happens through new experiences.** Knowing why you check locks doesn't stop the checking. But noticing yourself checking—creating that observer awareness—begins to build new neural pathways alongside the old ones.

The Observer and the Pattern

Right now, as you read this, try something: Notice your shoulders. Are they tense? Raised? Now notice who's doing the noticing. The part of you that can observe "my shoulders are tense" isn't tense itself—it's just watching.

That observer has been there all along. It's what neuroscientists call metacognitive awareness—your capacity to be aware of your own mental and physical states. When anxiety runs, the observer can watch it. When you check locks, the observer can notice. This isn't dissociation or leaving your body—it's expanding your awareness to include both the experience and the witnessing of it.

Some days you'll be 99% pattern, 1% observer. Other days maybe 90/10. The percentages don't matter. What matters is that any percentage of observer changes the experience from unconscious to conscious.

What This Means for Your Patterns

Your patterns developed for good reasons:

- Checking kept something safe once
- Scanning helped you avoid danger
- Leaving your body helped you survive overwhelming experiences
- Saying yes kept connections that mattered

These aren't character flaws or weaknesses. They're creative adaptations to challenging circumstances. Your nervous system did what it needed to do. Some patterns might still be protecting you from real, current threats. If you live in an actually unsafe neighborhood, hypervigilance makes sense. If you're in an abusive relationship, your body's alarm signals are accurate. Not every pattern needs updating—sometimes your body knows exactly what it's doing.

The question isn't **"How do I get rid of these patterns?"** but **"How do I develop awareness of them?"** With awareness comes choice—not always, not immediately, but sometimes. And sometimes is enough to begin changing lifelong patterns.

Remember This

Your patterns are survival strategies, not character defects. They protected you once—maybe they still do. The goal isn't to eliminate them but to see them clearly.

You have anxiety sometimes, but you're also the part that notices anxiety. You have patterns, but you're also the observer of those patterns. That observer has always been there, waiting patiently for you to notice it noticing.

Some days the patterns will run completely, no observer in sight. That's normal. Building metacognitive awareness is like learning any skill—inconsistent at first, stronger with practice.

Tomorrow you might catch yourself mid-pattern and think, "Oh, there it is." That moment of recognition—however brief—is everything. Not because it stops the pattern but because it reminds you: you are more than your automatic responses.

Even reading this chapter and occasionally thinking "I do that" or "that's not me" means your observer is active. You're already building the awareness that makes choice possible.

KEY TERMS TO REMEMBER

Observer Capacity

The part of you that can notice what you're thinking or feeling without being completely consumed by it. Some people call it awareness; some call it the witness; some call it the prefrontal cortex doing its job.

Protective Patterns

Behaviors your body learned to keep you safe, which might keep running even when you don't need them anymore. Like a smoke alarm that goes off when you make toast.

Hypervigilance

Being on high alert all the time, constantly scanning for danger even when things are safe. Your internal security guard who won't take a break.

* * *

Next: Chapter 1 Practice
Simple exercises to notice patterns without trying to change them

CHAPTER 1 PRACTICE

You're Not Broken

Simply notice your patterns. Don't try to change them.

* * *

Understanding the Shift

Before you practice, notice the difference between these two ways of relating to patterns:

Identification with Pattern	Observer Awareness
"I am anxious"	"I notice anxiety is present"
"I'm a checker"	"I observe checking behavior arising"
"I can't handle stress"	"I notice my system responding to stress"
"I'm broken"	"I have patterns that once protected me"

This shift in language is the foundation for everything that follows.

Quick Body Scan

Right now, without changing anything:

Shoulders:

_____

Jaw:

_____

Breath:

_____

Stomach:

_____

The part of you noticing the tension—is IT tense? No? That's your observer. It's always calm, just watching.

Today's Pattern Tracking

Watch for these common patterns (check any you notice):

- ☐ Checking locks/stove/doors multiple times

- ☐ Scanning for exits or tracking everyone's mood

- ☐ Leaving your body when stressed

- ☐ Pulling back from good things

- ☐ Physical symptoms when emotionally upset

When you catch a pattern, try saying:

"Oh, there's my [checking/scanning/leaving] pattern. Hello, old friend."

Pattern I caught today:

_____

Quick Origins Check

Without analyzing, just wonder: When might this pattern have first helped you?

_____

_____

Sometimes you'll know. Sometimes you won't. Both are fine.

* * *

Tonight's Reflection

Before bed, complete this one observation:

Today I noticed myself:

_____

and instead of fighting it, I:

_____

_____

KEY TAKEAWAY

I have anxiety sometimes,

but I'm also the part that notices the anxiety.

That noticing part has been here all along.

Remember: Noticing IS the practice. That's it. That's enough.

* * *

Next: Chapter 2 — Your Inner Protector
We'll explore why you might pull back from good things right before they bloom

CHAPTER 2

Your Inner Protector

When good things feel dangerous

* * *

> **Today's Focus**
>
> *Notice when you want to back away from something good. Just notice the urge.*

Your First Recognition

Think of the last time something genuinely good was about to happen to you. A job offer. Someone saying "I love you." An opportunity to share your work. Did your first instinct include any of these?

- Immediate need to minimize it ("It's not that great")
- Physical contraction or backing away
- Searching for what's wrong with it
- Urge to say no before thinking it through
- Feeling like you're about to be "found out"

If yes, your inner protector was activating. Let's understand why.

THE PATTERN

Sometimes the promotion arrives and something in us recoils. Not always from past trauma— sometimes from reasonable fear.

The responsibility feels too heavy. The spotlight too bright. We question if we've fooled them, if we can sustain the facade.

Or maybe good things did turn bad before— success brought someone's rage, happiness triggered chaos, love came with a price.

So now we might pull back, might sabotage, might run.

Or maybe we're just being careful, having learned to read the signs.

Last week, I was offered a chance to lead a workshop on this very material—the patterns I've spent years understanding. Two hundred people wanting to learn what I know. My first thought wasn't excitement. It was: "They're going to realize I'm making this up as I go."

My second thought: "I should cancel before they figure it out."

My third thought: "Oh, there's my inner protector, right on schedule."

I've sabotaged enough opportunities to recognize the pattern. The urge to pull back from good things isn't random. It's protective. The question is: protecting from what?

Not Everyone Has This Pattern

Some people embrace good things naturally. Promotion? Wonderful. New relationship? Let's see where it goes. Success? They celebrate without waiting for the other shoe to drop.

If that's you, this chapter might feel foreign. That's valuable information about your nervous system—it doesn't code "good" as "dangerous."

But for many of us, good things trigger the same alarm system as threats. We pull back, minimize, sabotage, or run. Not because we're self-destructive, but because our protective system is doing exactly what it learned to do.

* * *

The Core Truth: Protection Disguised as Sabotage

What looks like self-sabotage is often self-protection. Your inner protector isn't trying to ruin your life—it's trying to save you from dangers it perceives, whether they're real or remembered.

Just like in Chapter 1, where we learned to observe patterns rather than be consumed by them, here we're learning to recognize our protective responses to good things. The pull-back isn't a character flaw. It's your nervous system saying: "I remember when good things turned dangerous."

Kyle's TV Network Opportunity

A few months ago, Kyle got an opportunity to partner with a friend and build a TV network. Real funding. Real potential. The kind of opportunity he'd talked about for years.

Kyle: "Mom, James wants me to partner on this streaming platform."

Me: "That's incredible! This is what you've been working toward."

Kyle: "Yeah." (long pause) "I don't know if I should do it."

Me: "What's the hesitation?"

Kyle: "Everything. What if I can't deliver? What if the friendship gets ruined? What if I'm not actually good enough to pull this off?"

Me: "Your inner protector just activated."

Kyle: "My what?"

Me: "The part of you that pulls back from good things. I have it too. Remember when I almost didn't set aside the time to write this book?"

Kyle: "You kept saying you were too busy with your practice."

Me: "Right. Same pattern. The protector sees opportunity and immediately sees danger—exposure, failure, disappointment. It's trying to protect us from those possibilities."

Kyle: "By making me throw away the actual opportunity?"

Me: "By keeping you safe from what it thinks might happen. Your protector remembers every time standing out meant criticism. Every time success brought pressure. Every time 'good' turned complicated."

Kyle: "So what did you do with the book?"

Me: "I noticed the pattern. Said 'thank you for trying to protect me' to that part of myself. Then I looked at what was actually true—was this real danger or remembered danger?"

Kyle: "And?"

Me: "Both, honestly. Writing a book is genuinely risky—people might hate it, criticize it, reject it. But the danger my protector was responding to was mostly old—fear of being seen, of not being perfect, of disappointing people. Those were childhood dangers, not current ones."

Kyle spent three weeks in paralysis about the opportunity. Started to ghost James rather than give an answer. Classic protector move—if you disappear, you can't fail or be rejected.

Finally, Kyle examined what his protector was actually protecting him from:

- Fear of losing the friendship if business went bad (reasonable concern)
- Fear of public failure (possible but survivable)
- Fear of success making him a target (old pattern from family dynamics)
- Fear of not being able to maintain success (perfectionism)

Some were current, legitimate concerns worth considering. Others were old programs running on outdated information.

Why Your Protector Activates

Your inner protector might pull you back from good things for several reasons:

Past Association: If good things previously led to pain, your nervous system bookmarked "good = danger":

- Childhood success triggered parent's jealousy or rage
- Standing out meant becoming a target
- Happiness was followed by loss
- Achievement brought impossible expectations

Imposter Syndrome: Studies suggest approximately 70% of people experience feeling like a fraud at some point. Your protector might be trying to save you from being "exposed":

- "They'll realize I don't know what I'm doing"
- "I fooled them but I can't keep it up"
- "I don't deserve this and they'll figure it out"

Visibility Fears: Good things often mean being seen:

- More eyes on you means more judgment
- Success makes you a target for criticism
- Being visible means you can't hide flaws

Perfectionism: If you believe you must be perfect to deserve good things:

- Success means pressure to maintain impossible standards
- One mistake could ruin everything
- Better to not try than to try and fail

Legitimate Intuition: Sometimes your protector is right:

- The opportunity genuinely isn't aligned with your values
- Your body senses red flags your mind hasn't recognized
- The timing actually is wrong
- The cost truly is too high

The Difference Between Protection and Wisdom

This is crucial: not every pull-back is trauma response. Sometimes your protector is giving you accurate, current information. The practice is learning to tell the difference.

Signs it might be old protection:

- Immediate, intense physical reaction disproportionate to situation
- Familiar feeling you've had many times before
- Can't articulate specific current concerns
- Fear is about what "might" happen based on what did happen
- Pattern repeats across different situations

Signs it might be current wisdom:

- Specific, articulable concerns about this situation
- Body feels grounded, not panicked
- Can identify actual red flags or misalignments
- Decision comes from assessment, not fear
- Pattern is specific to this type of situation

Kyle's situation had both. The fear of ruining the friendship was current wisdom—business partnerships can strain friendships. But the terror of being "exposed" as incompetent? That was old protection from years of feeling like he had to be perfect to be valued.

Working With Your Protector

Remember from Chapter 1: awareness creates choice. You can't work with a pattern you don't acknowledge. The same applies here.

When you notice yourself pulling back from something good:

- **First, recognize it:** "Oh, my inner protector is activating."
- **Second, thank it:** "Thank you for trying to keep me safe."
- **Third, get curious:** "What danger are you protecting me from?"
- **Fourth, assess:** "Is this current danger or remembered danger?"
- **Fifth, choose:** "What do I need right now?"

Sometimes you'll choose to pull back anyway. That's not failure—it's conscious choice instead of unconscious pattern.

What Kyle Chose

After recognizing his pattern, Kyle did something interesting. He proposed a trial partnership with James—three months to test the waters. This honored both his protector's concerns (not fully committing) and his desire for the opportunity (not fully retreating).

"I told James I needed to start small," Kyle told me. "That I wanted to protect our friendship while exploring the business. He actually appreciated the caution."

This is the key: Kyle's protector wasn't wrong to be cautious. It just needed updating about what cautions were currently relevant versus which were ghosts from the past.

Three months in, the partnership is working. Not perfectly—there have been challenges. But Kyle's conscious choice to proceed carefully served him better than either jumping in blindly or running away entirely.

Your Pattern of Protection

Right now, think about the last opportunity you pulled back from. Can you feel your protector's presence in that decision?
Maybe it saved you from something genuinely misaligned. Maybe it protected you from a danger that no longer exists. Maybe both.

The point isn't to override your protector. It's to understand what it's protecting you from, so you can make conscious choices about what protection you actually need.

Remember This

Your inner protector developed for good reasons. Every time you pull back from good things, you're not being self-destructive—you're being self-protective based on what you've learned.
The tragedy isn't that you have this protection. It's when the protection runs on outdated information, keeping you from good things that are actually safe now.

Like Kyle learning to examine his hesitation about the TV network, you can learn to dialogue with your protector. Not to eliminate it—it might be right sometimes. But to understand it, update it, and choose consciously whether to follow its guidance.

Tomorrow you might notice yourself pulling back from a compliment, an opportunity, or someone's affection. Instead of judging yourself for sabotaging, try getting curious: "What is my protector trying to save me from?"

The answer might surprise you. And that awareness might be all you need to choose differently—or to choose the same thing but consciously, knowing why.

KEY TERMS TO REMEMBER

Inner Protector
The part of you that pulls back from good things to keep you safe from real or remembered dangers. Not a saboteur—a bodyguard working with outdated information.

Protective Hesitation
The pause or pull-back before good things that might be old fear, current wisdom, or both. Your system's way of saying "wait, let me check if this is safe."

Imposter Syndrome
The feeling that you're a fraud who will be "found out," even when you've earned your success. Approximately 70% of people experience this at some point.

Conscious Retreat
Choosing to pull back from an opportunity after examining whether the danger is current or remembered. Not self-sabotage, but self-care based on present assessment.

* * *

Next: Chapter 2 Practice

Your workbook exercises to explore your response to good things

CHAPTER 2 PRACTICE

Your Inner Protector

Notice when you pull back from good things. Get curious about what you're being protected from.

* * *

Quick Pattern Recognition

Think of a recent good thing (opportunity, compliment, relationship progress) that made you want to pull back.

The good thing was: _____

My first instinct was to:

☐   Minimize it

☐   Find what's wrong with it

☐   Run from it

☐   Sabotage it

☐   Disappear

☐   Other: _____

Whatever you checked—that's information, not judgment

* * *

Protection Investigation

What might my protector be trying to save me from?

- ☐ Being seen/exposed

- ☐ Disappointment (mine or others')

- ☐ Not being able to maintain it

- ☐ Success bringing problems

- ☐ History repeating

- ☐ Actual current red flags

- ☐ Other: _____

Old Protection vs. Current Wisdom

For the situation above, sort your concerns:

Feels like OLD protection (from past):

_____

Feels like CURRENT wisdom (about now):

_____

Not sure which:

_____

Dialogue with Your Protector

If your protector could speak, what would it say? "I'm trying to protect you from _____ "

Your response: "Thank you for _____ " "What I need you to know about now vs. then: _____ "

Today's Practice

When something good happens today (even tiny things):

1. Notice your first impulse
2. If you feel pull-back, pause
3. Say internally: "Hello, protector. What are you worried about?"
4. Listen without judgment
5. Thank it for trying to keep you safe

Tonight's Reflections

One good thing I noticed myself pulling back from:

_____

What my protector might have been worried about:

_____

Whether that worry was current or old:

_____

KEY TAKEAWAY

My inner protector isn't trying to sabotage me. It's trying to save me from dangers it remembers. Some of those dangers are gone now. I can thank my protector and update it about what's actually true today.

Remember: Sometimes pulling back IS wisdom. The practice is becoming conscious of why.

* * *

Next: Chapter 3 — The Body's Memory

Why your body holds what your mind forgets

CHAPTER 3

When Your Body Speaks

Understanding physical symptoms as communication

* * *

Today's Focus

Your body holds what your mouth couldn't say. The symptoms are real, even when the cause is emotional.

Some of us recognize this ledger immediately. Our bodies are walking inventories of everything we couldn't express. Others have never connected their migraines to their silences, their back pain to their burdens. Both responses are normal.

Scan your body right now: Where do you hold tension? What part hurts most often?

When did it start? Just notice. Don't try to fix or release anything. Your body keeps a ledger of everything you couldn't express. Let's explore what this means.

THE BODY'S LEDGER

Monday: stood silent while he screamed.

Tuesday: migraine, left side only.

Wednesday: smiled through the meeting

where they cut my hours.

Thursday: back spasms—can't stand straight.

Friday: Mom calls me ungrateful.

Saturday: stomach cramps so sharp

I fold on the bathroom tile.

The doctor finds nothing.

Labs perfect. Scans clean.

"Try yoga," she says. "Reduce stress."

My jaw aches with words I never said.

My shoulders hold ten years of swallowed comebacks.

My stomach works on rage I pushed down with dinner.

Research on psychosomatic symptoms confirms: Physical symptoms from emotional causes are measurably real.

This helped me understand that my symptoms weren't "just in my head." But before we go further, let me be clear: Physical symptoms have many possible contributors: genetics, injury, infection, autoimmune conditions, environmental factors, AND sometimes emotional stress. We're exploring just one piece of a complex puzzle, not the whole picture.

What I'm sharing here is specifically about that emotional piece— when and how it might play a role. This isn't about replacing medical investigation or claiming all symptoms are emotional. It's about understanding one factor that sometimes contributes to physical symptoms.

Let me be crystal clear: Pain is pain. Exhaustion is exhaustion. When I say stress causes physical symptoms, I'm not saying they're imaginary. They're measurably, physically real. Your body doesn't distinguish between physical and emotional threats—it responds with actual, physical changes either way.

This is why awareness matters: your body has been trying to tell you something. Maybe for years. Before we can work with symptoms, we need to acknowledge them. Just like in previous chapters—awareness first, then understanding, then gentle experiments. Your body won't release what hasn't been recognized.

When you can't express anger, your muscles tense as if preparing to fight. That tension is real—you can measure it with instruments. When you suppress grief, your body carries it like actual weight. Chronic stress produces inflammatory chemicals that create genuine symptoms: disrupted digestion (that's your actual gut bacteria changing), muscle tension (real muscle fibers contracting), compromised immunity (measurable drops in immune function).

Your body developed this vocabulary when words weren't safe or available. That conference call triggers migraines—real ones, with real blood vessel changes. Your mother's voice tightens your chest—actual muscle contraction you could see on a scan. Sunday nights hurt your stomach—genuine digestive disruption. Your body keeps score of patterns your conscious mind might miss.

Last week I had a crushing headache after a phone call with a family member. Nothing dramatic happened in the call. But my body was screaming about all the things I didn't say. The headache was real—throbbing, nauseating, lasted six hours. The cause was emotional. Both things are true.

Kyle's Pattern Discovery: An Illustration

Kyle had been getting migraines for months with no clear medical cause. This teaching example shows how body patterns sometimes reveal themselves through observation:

Terrell: "You've had four migraines this month?"

Kyle: "Yeah. MRI clean, blood work perfect. Doctor says 'reduce stress.'"

Terrell: "Let's track when they happen. What about the last one?"

Kyle: "Monday morning."

Terrell: "What happened Sunday?"

Kyle: "Weekly call with Mom."

Over several weeks of tracking, Kyle began noticing a pattern:

- Migraines often followed family calls where he didn't express his actual feelings
- They appeared after work meetings where he agreed to things he didn't want to do
- They came after conversations with his girlfriend where he suppressed his concerns

Kyle: "So basically, when I don't speak up, I get a migraine?"

Terrell: "That's what the pattern suggests."

Kyle later told me: "My dentist had been telling me I was clenching my jaw for years. Now I realize I'm literally biting back words."

This illustrative example shows how symptoms sometimes—not always—correlate with emotional suppression. Kyle's pattern won't be everyone's pattern. But the practice of noticing connections can be revealing.

Patterns Some People Report

Many people notice their bodies tend to hold tension in specific areas during emotional stress. These are patterns some practitioners and individuals have observed, though everyone's body responds uniquely:

Common patterns people report:

- Jaw tension when holding back words or anger
- Throat tightness when unable to express needs
- Shoulder tension when feeling burdened or responsible
- Chest tightness during grief or heartbreak

- Stomach issues when "digesting" difficult emotions
- Lower back pain during times of feeling unsupported
- Hip tension that some associate with stored trauma

Important: These are observations, not universal rules. Your body has its own unique mapping. Some people carry stress in completely different ways. There's no "right" or "wrong" place to hold tension.

My personal experience? Jaw tension when I'm angry (my dentist can always tell when I'm stressed). Shoulders up at my ears when overwhelmed. Lower back pain during periods of feeling unsupported. It took me forty years to notice these connections, and they're specific to me.

Why Your Body Reacts This Way

I spent months diving into research on this, partly to understand my own symptoms, partly to help Kyle understand his. Here's what the evidence shows:

What research tells us clearly:

The gut-brain connection is real: Your gut contains about 500 million neurons—more than in your spinal cord. Scientists call it the "enteric nervous system." While 90% of the body's serotonin is produced in the gut, this serotonin doesn't cross into the brain to affect mood directly. Instead, the gut and brain communicate through other neural and chemical pathways.

This is why digestive issues and emotional states are often linked.

Emotional suppression and inflammation: Some research has found associations between emotional suppression and inflammatory markers, though individual responses vary greatly. Chronic inflammation can contribute to various physical symptoms, from pain to fatigue.

What clinical observations suggest:

Many practitioners report patterns they've observed:

- Clients who struggle with boundaries often report more headaches
- Many chronic pain patients recall significant stressors before pain onset
- Some people experience symptom relief after learning to express emotions

Important caveat: These are observations and correlations, not proven causation. Every person is unique. What's consistent is that stress-related physical symptoms are real and measurable, regardless of their exact mechanism.

What This Means for You

Rather than seeing these as fixed rules, consider them invitations to curiosity:

- If you have chronic symptoms, might there be an emotional component worth exploring?
- If you frequently suppress feelings, what might your body be holding?
- If certain situations trigger physical symptoms, what pattern might be revealing itself?

Not every physical symptom has an emotional cause, and not every emotional stress creates physical symptoms. But understanding the connection can open new paths to relief.

My migraines didn't magically disappear when I understood they followed suppressed anger. But now I can sometimes catch myself clenching my jaw before the migraine starts. Sometimes I can speak up instead of swallowing words. Sometimes.

Important Medical Note

Always consult healthcare providers first for any persistent or concerning physical symptoms. This chapter explores one potential factor in physical symptoms, not the only factor. Medical evaluation is essential to rule out physical causes. The practices below are meant to complement, never replace, professional medical care.

Today's Practices

From research on somatic awareness: Different approaches work for different types of body tension. Based on what I read about body-based practices, I experimented with these variations.

Choose ONE that matches where you hold tension:

The Symptom Timeline

Track what happened 24-48 hours before symptoms. Who were you with? What couldn't you say? What did you swallow instead?

Why this works: You start seeing connections between suppression and symptoms.

The Body Check-In

Three times today, pause and ask: "What is my jaw doing? My shoulders? My stomach?" Don't change anything, just notice. Awareness first—your body needs witness before willingness.

Why this works: Awareness of tension is the first step to releasing it.

The Translation Practice

When symptoms arise, ask: "If this pain could speak, what would it say?" Write the first thing that comes. Don't edit.

Why this works: Your body often knows what your mind won't admit.

The One-Minute Voice

Set a timer. Say out loud (alone) everything you couldn't say today. Let it be messy, angry, sad. Your body needs to hear your voice speaking truth.

Why this works: Physical expression releases what silence stores.

Yesterday I tried the one-minute voice after a frustrating call.61 Stood in my car and said everything I'd swallowed. Felt ridiculous. Looked ridiculous. But the tension in my shoulders dropped. Not completely, but noticeably.

Remember This

- Physical symptoms from emotional stress are real and measurable
- The gut contains about 500 million neurons—a "second brain"
- Stress affects inflammation, which can create genuine symptoms
- Body-emotion patterns vary widely between individuals
- Some people experience symptom relief when expressing suppressed emotions
- Medical evaluation remains essential for physical symptoms
- These are patterns to explore, not universal rules

Your body isn't betraying you. It's been loyally holding everything you couldn't express, storing what you couldn't process, saying what you couldn't voice.

Remember: This understanding complements, not replaces, medical care. Always consult healthcare providers for persistent or concerning symptoms. But if they say "it's stress" and send you home, now you have some tools to work with that stress.

My body still holds things. Right now my shoulders are creeping up as I write about this. Old pattern. But I notice it now. Sometimes I can release it. Sometimes I can't. Both are okay.

KEY TERMS TO REMEMBER

Enteric Nervous System
The network of about 500 million neurons in your gut, often called the "second brain." When people say "gut feeling," they're more right than they know.

Somatic Symptoms
Physical symptoms that arise from emotional or psychological stress rather than physical injury or illness. Real symptoms, emotional cause.

Body Mapping
The unique way your individual body stores and expresses emotional experiences through physical sensations. Your personal symptom dictionary.

Inflammatory Response
The body's physical reaction to stress that can create real, measurable symptoms including pain and fatigue. Not imaginary, actually happening in your tissues.

Next: Chapter 3 Practice
Your body holds what your mouth couldn't say

CHAPTER 3 PRACTICE

When Your Body Speaks
Your body holds what your mouth couldn't say

* * *

Quick Body Scan

Check each area right now. Don't change anything, just notice:

- ☐ Jaw: Tight or relaxed?

- ☐ Shoulders: At ears or dropped?

- ☐ Stomach: Knotted or calm?

- ☐ Back: Tense or supported?

- ☐ Breath: Shallow or deep?

Just observing. Not changing. Just noticing.

* * *

The Symptom Timeline

Think of a recent physical symptom:

What symptom appeared:

_____

What happened 24-48 hours before:

_____

What I couldn't say or express:

_____

KEY TAKEAWAY

*My body isn't my enemy. It's been loyally holding what
I couldn't express. Every symptom is a message.
Every pain has logic. I'm learning to listen.*

Your body deserves curiosity, not anger.

* * *

Next: Chapter 4 — Finding One Safe Place
When the house of your body feels haunted

CHAPTER 4

Finding One Safe Place

When the house of your body feels haunted

* * *

I'm sitting in my therapist's office. She says, "Let's do a body scan to help you relax."

My internal response: *Are you kidding me?*

My chest is where panic lives. My throat closes when I try to speak truth. My stomach has been clenched since childhood. My shoulders are permanently braced for impact. Scanning my body isn't relaxing—it's touring a war zone.

"I can't," I tell her. "Every part of my body is screaming."

"Then let's find just one part that isn't," she says.

This is how I learned that when your entire body feels like enemy territory, you don't need to make peace with all of it. You just need to find one neutral zone. One tiny spot that proves not everything is dangerous.

ONE QUIET ROOM

"Scan your body," she says.
I float somewhere near the ceiling instead,
watching from a safer distance.

Shoulders: holding something heavy.
Chest: breathing carefully.
Stomach: tight with old caution.

Feel your body, they say.
But feeling means remembering,
and remembering means landing
where I learned to leave.

Today I wonder about my knees.
Nothing stored there—just bone and skin.
My pinky finger: unremarkable, quiet.
Small places that feel... empty of story.

I don't need the whole house yet.
Just one room where I can sit
without listening for footsteps.

When Awareness Itself Feels Dangerous

In the previous chapters, you've been developing awareness:

- **Chapter 1:** You learned you HAVE patterns rather than BEING them

- **Chapter 2:** You recognized protection disguised as self-sabotage

- **Chapter 3:** You discovered your body holds what couldn't be expressed

But what if every attempt at awareness feels overwhelming? What if noticing your body means noticing pain, tension, trauma memories? What if the instruction "observe your anxiety" is impossible because your entire body IS anxiety?

This chapter is for when awareness itself feels dangerous. When your body feels like enemy territory you can't escape.

When Bodies Become Battlegrounds

Your body might feel like enemy territory if you've experienced:

Trauma that lives in your skin: Sexual assault survivors often describe their bodies as crime scenes they can't leave. Every sensation might trigger memories. The body that was violated doesn't feel like home anymore.

Chronic pain that won't stop: When pain has been constant for months or years, your body becomes the source of suffering. Every movement hurts. Your body feels like it's attacking you from the inside.

Panic that makes your body feel lethal: During panic attacks, your body feels like it's trying to kill you. Between attacks, you monitor every sensation suspiciously, waiting for the next assault from within.

Medical trauma: Multiple surgeries, invasive procedures, or medical emergencies can make your body feel like a thing that gets done to, not a safe place to inhabit.

Childhood that required hypervigilance: If you grew up needing to constantly monitor for danger, your body might still be on duty decades later, unable to stand down.

Finding the First Safe Zone

When Kyle tried body scanning in therapy, he found only activation everywhere—headache in his temples, can't breathe in his chest, nausea in his stomach, legs that wanted to run. His therapist suggested something different: "Find just one boring spot. Something that feels like nothing special."

His right elbow. That was it. Normal, boring, unremarkable.

"That's ridiculous," he told me later. "How is my elbow supposed to help with panic?"

"Your elbow is proof that not everything in your body is in crisis," I explained. "It's one spot that isn't at war."

This small shift—from needing the whole body to calm down to finding just one neutral spot—changes everything. You don't need your entire body to feel safe. You just need one tiny zone that remembers what "okay" feels like.

Why One Safe Zone Changes Everything

Remember in Chapter 1 when we discovered the observer—the part of you that notices patterns without being consumed by them? When your whole body feels like enemy territory, you can't access that observer. You're too consumed by the sensations.

But finding one neutral spot changes everything:

The neutral spot IS your observer's home base.

When you notice "my elbow feels okay," WHO is noticing? The observer. And where can the observer rest its attention without getting pulled into activation? That neutral elbow.

This is awareness at its most basic and crucial:

- Not awareness of complex patterns
- Not awareness of emotional nuance
- Just awareness that one tiny part of you is okay

Understanding Your Body's Internal Sensing

Interoception is your ability to sense what's happening inside your body—hunger, thirst, heartbeat, breathing, internal pain or comfort. It's how you know you need to eat, rest, or use the bathroom. It's also how you sense emotions, which often appear first as body sensations.

Why this matters for finding neutral zones:

When interoception works well: You can accurately sense different body states. You know when you're hungry versus anxious, tired versus sad. You can find and recognize neutral spots easily.

When trauma disrupts interoception: You might experience:

- **Hypersensitivity:** Every sensation feels overwhelming or dangerous. Your heartbeat feels like panic. Normal digestion feels like illness.

- **Hyposensitivity:** You can't feel much at all. You might not notice hunger, pain, or exhaustion until they're extreme.

- **Inaccuracy:** You misread signals. Anxiety feels like hunger. Exhaustion feels like depression.

Finding one neutral spot helps recalibrate interoception because:

- It gives your nervous system a reference point for "calm"
- It proves you can accurately identify at least one sensation
- It builds trust between your conscious awareness and body signals
- It creates a baseline from which to notice other sensations

Without basic interoceptive awareness, you can't tell if you're improving or getting worse, can't identify what your body needs, and can't use body-based healing approaches. The neutral spot is your entry point to rebuilding accurate body sensing.

Building Your Neutral Map

Start with finding just one neutral or boring spot. Common ones people discover:

Often neutral zones:

- Earlobes (rarely hold tension)
- Elbows or knees (practical, boring joints)
- Pinky fingers or toes (often forgotten by trauma)
- The space between fingers
- Behind the ears
- Palm centers (unless you clench fists)

Important: Your neutral map is unique. Where one person finds calm in their feet, another might find their feet hold old fear. There's no wrong answer—only what's true for your body.

How Awareness Grows from One Spot

Kyle started with just his elbow. Here's how his awareness developed over several weeks:

Week 1: "During panic, I remembered my elbow exists and is calm." (Tiny awareness during overwhelming activation)

Week 2: "I can feel my elbow while my chest is tight." (Awareness of both neutral and activated simultaneously)

Week 3: "The tight chest is 90% of my experience, the calm elbow is 10%." (The observer from Chapter 1 is now quantifying, not drowning)

Week 4: "I am having panic AND I have a calm elbow." (The core realization from Chapter 1—having versus being—now anchored in physical sensation)

Kyle still has panic attacks. But now there's always 1% of him—the part aware of the neutral elbow—that isn't consumed by them. That 1% is everything.

Daily Life with One Safe Zone

Morning: Wake up, anxiety already running. Before getting out of bed, find your neutral spot. "My knee is okay." That's your awareness practice. That's enough.

Commute: Crowded train, panic rising. Touch your earlobe. "This part is fine." You're still anxious, but not 100% consumed.

Work presentation: Heart pounding, hands shaking. Under the table, press your neutral knee. Remember: "Not all of me is panicking."

Night: Can't sleep, body won't calm down. Find your neutral spot. Don't try to spread the calm. Just know: "This one part of me is already at rest."

When This Practice Isn't Right

This practice might not serve you if:

- Focusing on any body part increases dissociation
- You have active psychosis or severe PTSD (work with a professional)
- Body focus triggers eating disorder behaviors
- You're in acute crisis (seek immediate support)

Alternative: If body focus doesn't work, try external anchors:

- A smooth stone in your pocket
- The temperature of your coffee cup
- The texture of fabric
- The sound of your own humming

The Bridge to Part Two

This chapter is the bridge between Part One's awareness and Part Two's practices. You can't do Part Two's movement and regulation practices if you have nowhere safe to start from. The neutral spot becomes:

- Your checkpoint between window and keyhole days (Chapter 5)
- Your anchor when anxiety is overwhelming (Chapter 6)
- Your proof of safety when your body won't rest (Chapter 7)
- Your starting point for movement (Chapter 8)

Without this chapter, readers whose bodies feel completely activated have no entry point to the practices. But "find one boring spot"? That's doable. That's the tiniest possible doorway into awareness.

Remember This

Finding one neutral spot in a body that feels like enemy territory isn't about healing trauma or stopping symptoms. It's about proving that not everything in your body is dangerous.

That proof—that tiny evidence of safety—becomes the seed from which larger awareness can grow. You don't need your whole body to feel safe. You just need one boring, neutral, reliable spot that reminds you: not everything is activated, not everything is traumatized, not everything is at war.

Sometimes that small reminder is all you need to get through the day. Sometimes it's the beginning of reclaiming your body as a safe place to exist. Either way, it's enough.

KEY TERMS TO REMEMBER

Neutral Zone
A spot in your body that doesn't carry trauma charge, chronic tension, or emotional activation. Boring is perfect.

Body as Enemy Territory
When trauma, pain, or chronic stress makes your entire body feel unsafe to inhabit.

Interoception
Your ability to sense internal body signals—hunger, thirst, heartbeat, pain, comfort. Trauma can make this system hyper- or hypo-sensitive. Finding neutral zones helps recalibrate it.

Anchor Point
The neutral spot that gives your observer a safe place to rest attention during activation.

Next: Chapter 4 Practice
Your gentle exploration of neutral spaces

CHAPTER 4 PRACTICE

Finding One Safe Place

When your whole body feels activated, find one spot that doesn't.

* * *

Initial Scan for Neutral

Without forcing, gently wonder about these areas:

☐ Right earlobe

☐ Left earlobe

☐ Right elbow

☐ Left elbow

☐ Right knee

☐ Left knee

☐ Pinky finger

☐ Space between fingers

☐ Behind ears

Mark any that feel neutral, boring, or "nothing special."

Your Safe Zone

My neutral spot is: _____

When I notice it, it feels: _____

Daily Check-In

Morning: Can I find my neutral spot? Yes / No

Afternoon: Can I notice it while activated? Yes / No

Evening: Is it still neutral? Yes / No

Building Awareness

Week 1: Just notice the neutral spot exists

Week 2: Notice it during mild activation

Week 3: Find it during stronger activation

Week 4: Can you find a second neutral spot?

Remember: If you can't find a neutral spot today, that's okay. Try again tomorrow. Sometimes it takes time for the body to reveal its safe zones.

* * *

Next: Part One Conclusion
What you might have observed and what doesn't need to be fixed

PART ONE CONCLUSION

What You've Built: The Foundation of Awareness

You began Part One with patterns running unconsciously—checking locks without noticing, pulling back from opportunities without knowing why, feeling physical symptoms without understanding their message, experiencing your body as enemy territory with no safe harbor.
Now you have something different: awareness.

Not perfect awareness. Not constant awareness. But moments—sometimes fleeting, sometimes sustained—where you observe rather than drown.

The Four Layers of Recognition

Through four chapters, you've built awareness in layers:

First, you discovered the observer (Chapter 1). That part of you that notices "I'm checking the locks again" without being consumed by the checking. You learned the profound difference between having anxiety and being anxiety. This observer—sometimes just 1% of your experience—changes everything.

Second, you recognized protection (Chapter 2). What looked like self-sabotage revealed itself as self-protection. Your inner protector pulling you back from good things isn't trying to ruin your life—it's trying to save you from remembered dangers. Now you can dialogue with this protector rather than being unconsciously controlled by it.

Third, you understood your body's language (Chapter 3). Those migraines, that back pain, the chronic jaw tension—your body has been speaking what your mouth couldn't say. The symptoms are real, even when the cause is emotional. Now you can begin to listen rather than just suffer.

Fourth, you found safety in small spaces (Chapter 4). When your entire body feels like enemy territory, you discovered you don't need to reclaim all of it. One neutral spot—an earlobe, an elbow—becomes proof that not everything is dangerous. From this tiny seed, larger awareness can grow.

Why These Four Matter Together

These aren't separate skills. They're facets of one fundamental capacity: **the ability to observe your experience while having it.**

- The observer (Ch 1) needs a safe place to rest its attention (Ch 4)
- The protector (Ch 2) speaks through the body's symptoms (Ch 3)
- The body's symptoms (Ch 3) make sense when you understand protection (Ch 2)
- The neutral zone (Ch 4) gives the observer (Ch 1) an anchor during activation

Together, they create what you need for Part Two: **enough awareness to work with your patterns rather than being run by them.**

What's Different Now

Before Part One, patterns just happened to you. Anxiety consumed you. Your body was either numb or screaming. Good things felt dangerous for reasons you couldn't explain.

Now—not always, but sometimes—you catch patterns in action. You notice your shoulders rising before the yes comes out. You feel your protector pulling back and can ask what it's protecting you from. You recognize your jaw clenching as unspoken words. You find your neutral elbow when panic rises.

These moments of recognition don't fix anything. The patterns still run. But now they run with a witness.

The Bridge to Part Two

Part One gave you awareness. Part Two will show you what to do with it.

Because now you can:

- Notice your capacity (window vs keyhole days) and adjust accordingly
- Recognize when anxiety is giving accurate information vs. replaying old threats
- Thank your night guard instead of fighting with insomnia
- Choose movement that matches your actual state rather than forcing what you think you "should" do

Without Part One's awareness, Part Two's practices would be just more things to fail at. With awareness, they become experiments in working with your nervous system rather than against it.

Your Current Capacity

Take a moment to acknowledge what you've built:

☐ I can sometimes notice patterns while they're happening

☐ I occasionally catch the difference between having and being

☐ I've found at least one neutral spot in my body

☐ I recognize that pulling back might be protection

☐ I understand my body might be holding unexpressed emotions

☐ I can observe even if I can't change

If you checked even one box, you have enough awareness to begin Part Two.

A Note on Progress

Kyle still checks locks. I still say yes when I mean no. We both still have panic attacks and migraines and nights when our bodies won't calm down.

But now, sometimes, we notice. We catch ourselves mid-pattern. We find our neutral spots. We thank our protectors. We listen to what our bodies are trying to say.

This noticing—inconsistent, imperfect, often after the fact—is not failure. It's the slow rewiring of patterns that took decades to form.

Before You Continue

Part Two will ask you to experiment with gentle adjustments—not to fix or eliminate patterns, but to work with them consciously. Every practice will follow the same sequence you've learned here:

1. Notice what's happening (awareness from Part One)
2. Validate why it makes sense
3. Try a tiny adjustment (new in Part Two)

If you're not ready for experiments, stay with Part One longer. There's no rush. Building awareness is lifelong work, not a stage to complete.

But if you're ready to explore what becomes possible when awareness meets action, Part Two awaits.

Remember: You don't need perfect awareness. You just need enough to occasionally notice what's happening. That occasional noticing is the doorway to everything that follows.

* * *

Next: Part Two
Introduction From awareness to gentle experimentation

Young Hearts,
Endless Dreams

JOHANSEN

PART TWO

LEARNING TO MOVE

Practical experiments for different body states

Part One taught you to notice. Now comes the question that probably brought you to this book: What do I actually DO when I notice?

You can observe yourself checking locks five times, but how do you stop at three? You notice your capacity is limited today, but how do you actually work with that? You recognize anxiety rising, but then what?

This is where most approaches fail. They jump straight to techniques— breathe deeply, think positively, just relax—without acknowledging what your body is experiencing. Your nervous system rejects help it hasn't asked for.

THE THREE-STEP DANCE

Notice first—

the shoulders climbing,

the breath holding,

the pattern running.

Validate second—

"This makes sense because..."

"My body learned this when..."

"It's trying to protect me from..."

Only then, the tiniest adjustment—

one breath deeper,

shoulders dropping half an inch,

feet finding floor.

Skip to step three

and the body rebels.

"You don't understand the danger!"

it screams, getting louder.

But acknowledge first?

"I see you, I hear you, you make sense"—

and sometimes, just sometimes,

the body softens enough to try.

Why Techniques Fail Without Acknowledgment

For years, I tried breathing exercises for anxiety. They made it worse. My body would tighten more, as if fighting the forced calm. Then a somatic therapist taught me to acknowledge first: "I'm anxious about tomorrow's presentation, and that makes complete sense because the stakes are real."

Same breathing technique. Completely different result.

The acknowledgment changed everything. My body felt heard. It stopped fighting. The breathing actually helped.

This is Part Two's foundation: **Your body needs to be heard before it will listen.**

The Three-Step Practice

Every technique in Part Two follows this sequence:

1. **NOTICE** (from Part One): "My shoulders are at my ears."
2. **VALIDATE** (new): "This makes sense because I'm about to see my mother who always criticizes me."
3. **TINY ADJUSTMENT** (new): "Let me drop them half an inch. Not relaxed, just slightly less armored."

Skip validation and the adjustment rarely works. Your body rebels against change it hasn't agreed to.

Why This Pattern Works

This approach combines insights from several areas of research:

Self-compassion research shows that acknowledging our struggles— rather than fighting them—actually increases our capacity for change.

Kristin Neff's studies demonstrate that self-validation correlates with better outcomes and greater motivation to improve.

Behavioral change studies from researchers like BJ Fogg at Stanford show that tiny, incremental adjustments stick better than forced dramatic changes. The brain's neuroplasticity responds more effectively to small, repeated changes than to overwhelming shifts.

Somatic therapy practices have long observed that when we acknowledge what the body is experiencing before trying to change it, resistance decreases. Clinical practice consistently shows this pattern, though the exact mechanisms are still being studied.

Anxiety research demonstrates that fighting symptoms often amplifies them, while acknowledgment can reduce their intensity. This is why acceptance-based therapies have gained traction—they work with the body's responses rather than against them.

The validation creates receptivity. The tiny adjustment respects the body's protective mechanisms. And when the body rejects an adjustment? That's valuable information about what's needed instead.

What You'll Find in Part Two: Awareness Enabling Movement

Chapter 5: When Your Capacity Changes Your awareness from Part One lets you recognize window days (lots of capacity) versus keyhole days (minimal capacity). Now you'll learn to move accordingly—scaling your actions to match your actual capacity rather than forcing yourself through what you think you "should" handle. The movement here is adjusting your life to your nervous system's reality.

Chapter 6: When Anxiety Makes Sense Using the observer capacity from Chapter 1, you can now notice when anxiety carries accurate information versus old patterns. This awareness lets you choose your response—when to move toward action the anxiety suggests versus when to soothe with calming practices. Your awareness determines which movement serves you.

Chapter 7: When Sleep Won't Come Remember finding your neutral zone in Chapter 4? That becomes your anchor when your night guard won't stand down. You'll learn to acknowledge your guard's vigilance (validation), then guide attention to your neutral spot—the smallest movement from activation toward rest. It's movement through acknowledgment, not force.

Chapter 8: Movement as Medicine All of Part One's awareness culminates here: recognizing your patterns (Ch 1), understanding protection (Ch 2), reading body signals (Ch 3), and finding safe zones (Ch 4) lets you accurately identify what movement medicine your body needs. Lightning state needs discharge movement. Stone state needs tiny movements. Your awareness tells you which.

Each chapter builds on your awareness to enable appropriate movement—not random techniques, but responses matched to what your nervous system actually needs in that moment. Without Part One's awareness, you couldn't accurately assess your state. Without accurate assessment, you can't choose the right movement. This is why Part Two is called "Learning to Move"—you're learning to move from awareness into action that matches your actual state.

The Difference from Part One

Part One was about recognition without action. Just noticing, no pressure to change.

Part Two adds gentle experiments—but only after acknowledgment. We're not forcing change. We're offering your nervous system options it can accept or refuse.

Think of it as a conversation:

- Part One: Learning to hear what your body is saying
- Part Two: Learning to respond in ways your body can receive

Managing Expectations

Some days these practices will help. Your anxiety might soften after acknowledgment. You might sleep after thanking your night guard. Movement might discharge the activation.

Other days, nothing helps. You'll notice, validate, try to adjust, and the pattern runs anyway. This isn't failure—it's information about your nervous system's current state.

Kyle tried the capacity practices from Chapter 5 last week. Recognized he was having a keyhole day. Validated why (poor sleep, work stress). Tried to adjust by canceling non-essentials. Still ended up overwhelmed by evening.

"Did I fail?" he asked.

"No. You stayed conscious while overwhelmed. That's different from drowning without awareness."

* * *

Next: Part Two Practice
Preparing to experiment with awareness first

PART TWO PRACTICE

Preparing to Learn to Move
Setting yourself up for experiments, not perfection

* * *

Your Current State Check

After Part One, where are you now?

- ☐ I notice my patterns more

- ☐ I'm ready to try experiments

- ☐ I'm curious but cautious

- ☐ I need to go slowly

- ☐ I'm overwhelmed

- ☐ I'm skeptical

- ☐ I'm hopeful

- ☐ Not sure yet

I was all of these at once when I started Part Two. Hopeful but skeptical. Ready but overwhelmed. That's normal.

* * *

Your Relationship with "Techniques"

What have you tried before that didn't work?

- ☐ Deep breathing exercises

- ☐ Meditation apps

- ☐ Exercise for anxiety

- ☐ Sleep hygiene rules

- ☐ Positive thinking

- ☐ Grounding techniques

- ☐ Forcing through anxiety

Other techniques I've tried: _____

If techniques haven't worked, it might be because they skipped acknowledgment. Part Two does the same techniques but adds the crucial first step: hearing what your body is saying.

What You Want from Part Two

I'm most curious about working with:

_____

What I hope might shift:

_____

What I'm not ready to change:

_____

Being honest about what you're not ready to change is important. I wasn't ready to stop checking locks. Still did Part Two. Some patterns stayed, some softened. Both outcomes were okay.

Your Capacity Right Now

Today feels like a:

- ☐ Window day (lots of capacity)

- ☐ Keyhole day (very little capacity)

- ☐ Somewhere in between

- ☐ Not sure

This matters because Part Two teaches you to work with your actual capacity, not what you think you should have. If today is a keyhole day, maybe save the experiments for tomorrow.

Permission Setting

Give yourself permission for Part Two:

- ☐ To try experiments that might not work
- ☐ To skip what doesn't fit
- ☐ To have days when nothing helps
- ☐ To notice without changing
- ☐ To make tiny movements
- ☐ To count surviving as success
- ☐ To forget the three-step pattern
- ☐ To need multiple attempts

I needed permission to fail at the experiments. Half of them didn't work for me. That wasn't failure—it was data about my nervous system. Some patterns are too deep, too protective, or too necessary to shift with these techniques alone. Sometimes validation helps, sometimes it doesn't change anything, and both outcomes are valid information.

Before You Turn to Chapter 5

One thing I want to remember about awareness first:

My intention for these experiments:

What support I might need:

Remember: Part Two might activate you. Reading about anxiety might make you anxious. Reading about insomnia might keep you awake. That's normal. Your nervous system is trying to understand these patterns by experiencing them.

When that happens, return to the foundation: just notice. "Oh, reading about anxiety is making me anxious. That's interesting." You don't have to fix it. Just notice it.

You're about to learn that techniques you've tried before might work when you add acknowledgment first. Or they might not. Both outcomes teach you something.

Take breaks when needed. Skip chapters that don't fit. Remember that not everything will help. That's not failure—it's learning what medicine your particular nervous system needs.

PART TWO KEY PRINCIPLE

Every technique I'll learn follows the same pattern:

FIRST: Notice what's happening
SECOND: Validate why it makes sense
ONLY THEN: Try a gentle adjustment

My body needs acknowledgment
before it will consider change.

Sometimes the acknowledgment alone
is the medicine I need.

* * *

Next: Chapter 5 — When Your Capacity Changes
Why yesterday's normal is today's impossible

CHAPTER 5

When Your Capacity Changes

Why yesterday's normal is today's impossible

* * *

Yesterday you presented to thirty executives, handled your mother's crisis call, and helped a friend move. Today, a text notification made you cry in the bathroom.

What happened? Did you suddenly become weak? Are you regressing?

No. Your capacity changed.

This is the first movement lesson of Part Two: learning to adjust your life to match your actual capacity, not the capacity you think you should have.

WINDOW AND KEYHOLE DAYS

Monday: window wide open.
I can take the noise, the news, the
friend who needs three hours to
process her breakup.
My capacity feels infinite.

Tuesday: window half-closed.
Choose carefully what enters.
Work yes, drama no.
One conversation, not three.

Wednesday: looking through a keyhole.
Everything is too much.
The doorbell is an assault.
Sunlight feels aggressive.
Someone breathing nearby uses
all my bandwidth.

Same person. Same life.
Different capacity.

Learning to honor the keyhole days
instead of forcing the window open.

Connecting Awareness to Movement

In Part One, you learned to observe your patterns without judgment. Now that awareness becomes practical: you can recognize your capacity state and move accordingly.

The awareness skills from Part One enable you to:

- Notice early signs of capacity shifts (from Chapter 1's observer training)
- Recognize when your protector is pulling back because you're depleted (Chapter 2)
- Feel your body's signals of overwhelm before you crash (Chapter 3)
- Find your neutral spot when capacity shrinks (Chapter 4)

Now in Part Two, you'll use this awareness to make different choices—to move through your day in ways that match your actual capacity.

Your Window of Tolerance

Psychologists call it your "window of tolerance"—the zone where you can handle stress without becoming overwhelmed or shutting down. Inside this window, you can think clearly, connect with others, solve problems. Outside it, you're in survival mode.

But here's what many don't emphasize enough: this window isn't fixed. It changes constantly based on multiple factors, and recognizing these changes through awareness is the first step to working with them.

What Changes Your Capacity

Your nervous system's capacity fluctuates based on:

Sleep debt accumulation: One bad night shrinks your window by 30-50%. Your prefrontal cortex—the part that helps you regulate—needs adequate sleep to function. Without it, you're operating with reduced emotional regulation capacity.

Stress hormone levels: Cortisol and adrenaline from yesterday's stress don't just disappear. They accumulate, narrowing your window until your body can process them out through rest or movement.

Anniversary reactions: Your body remembers dates even when your mind doesn't. The anniversary of losses, traumas, or significant changes can shrink capacity without conscious awareness.

Social battery depletion: Every interaction uses capacity. Introverts deplete faster in social situations; extroverts might deplete from too much alone time. Neither is better—just different capacity patterns. Hormonal fluctuations: Natural hormone cycles affect neurotransmitter production and nervous system regulation. This isn't weakness—it's biology affecting capacity.

Hormonal fluctuations: Natural hormone cycles affect neurotransmitter production and nervous system regulation. This isn't weakness—it's biology affecting capacity.

Recognizing Your Current State

Using your Part One awareness skills, you can now identify capacity states:

Window Day Signs:

- Your observer (Ch 1) easily notices patterns without being consumed
- Your body (Ch 3) feels relatively settled
- You can find multiple neutral spots (Ch 4), not just one
- Problems feel solvable rather than overwhelming
- You have energy for others' needs
- The three-step pattern (notice-validate-adjust) works smoothly

Keyhole Day Signs:

- Hard to access your observer—you're mostly consumed by experience
- Body symptoms flare (Ch 3)—headaches, stomach issues, tension
- Can barely find one neutral spot (Ch 4)
- Everything feels too much, too loud, too close
- No energy for others
- Even tiny adjustments feel impossible

An Illustration: Kyle's Capacity Crash

Kyle and his girlfriend Maddy had plans Tuesday evening. Monday, Kyle had handled everything brilliantly—work presentation, difficult client, even helped his coworker with a crisis.

Tuesday afternoon, Maddy texts about dinner.

> Kyle: "I can't do dinner out. I can barely do dinner at all."

> Maddy calls, confused: "But yesterday you were fine. You said you were looking forward to it."

> Kyle: "I was. Yesterday I had capacity. Today I don't."

> Maddy: "Did something happen?"

> Kyle: "Yes. I used all my capacity yesterday. Today's window is tiny. If I try to push through dinner out, I'll either shut down completely or snap at you over nothing."

This conversation shows the three-step pattern in action:

1. **Notice:** Kyle recognized his depleted state

2. **Validate:** "I used all my capacity yesterday"—acknowledgment without judgment
3. **Adjust:** Changing plans to match actual capacity

Maddy learning to not take Kyle's capacity changes personally was its own journey. But understanding that capacity fluctuates helped her see it wasn't about her or their relationship—it was about nervous system resources.

Working WITH Your Capacity: The Movement Practice

Here's where awareness becomes action. Instead of forcing yourself through a keyhole day with window-day expectations, you adjust:

On Window Days (wide capacity), you move expansively:

- Schedule challenging conversations
- Take on complex projects
- Offer support to others
- Try new experiences
- Use this capacity wisely—don't deplete it all
- Practice the adjustments from Part Two more boldly

On Keyhole Days (minimal capacity), you move minimally:

- Cancel non-essentials without guilt
- Communicate your limitations: "I'm having a limited capacity day"
- Do the bare minimum required
- Say no to additional requests
- Find your neutral spot (Ch 4) repeatedly
- Make only the tiniest adjustments, or just validate without adjusting

The key movement: Adjusting your actions to match your capacity IS the practice. This isn't giving up or being weak. It's conscious calibration.

The Validation Step Most People Skip

When you notice your capacity is limited, the immediate response is often self-criticism: "I should be able to handle this. I handled more yesterday."

But remember Part Two's foundation: validation before adjustment. Try this instead:

"My capacity is limited today. This makes complete sense because [I didn't sleep well/I'm still processing yesterday's stress/it's the anniversary of mom's death/my hormones are fluctuating/I've been in survival mode for weeks]."

Only after validation can you effectively adjust. Your nervous system needs to know you understand why it's struggling before it will accept modifications.

Capacity Debt and Recovery

Using all your window-day capacity creates what Kyle calls a "capacity hangover"—the next day (or several days) will likely be keyhole days.

This is your nervous system recovering, not you being weak. Just like muscles need recovery after intense exercise, your nervous system needs recovery after intense capacity use.

The movement practice here:

- **Plan for recovery:** If Monday is huge, keep Tuesday light
- **Communicate in advance:** "I have a big presentation Monday, so Tuesday I'll need a quiet day"

- **Resist guilt:** Recovery isn't laziness; it's necessary system maintenance

When Capacity Stays Low

Sometimes capacity remains limited for weeks or months. Chronic stress, ongoing trauma, illness, or major life changes can keep your window narrow long-term.

If this is you, the movement practice changes:

- Stop waiting for window days to live your life
- Learn to work within keyhole capacity
- Celebrate tiny accomplishments as major victories
- Adjust expectations to match reality
- Remember: managing with limited capacity takes MORE skill, not less

The Daily Practice

Each morning, use your awareness to assess capacity:

1. **Notice:** "Where's my capacity today?" Check your body signals, energy level, emotional resilience.
2. **Validate:** "This level makes sense because..." Always acknowledge why your capacity is where it is.
3. **Adjust:** "Based on this capacity, today I will..." Then actually adjust your day.

This isn't giving up on the day before it starts. It's conscious calibration that prevents crashes and honors your nervous system's reality.

Note: Your capacity might shift throughout the day. You might start with a window morning and crash into keyhole by afternoon, or vice versa. Consider checking at 2-3 transition points rather than assuming your morning capacity lasts all day. Many people find their capacity predictably shifts around the same times daily—learning your pattern helps you plan accordingly.

Remember This

Your changing capacity doesn't mean you're inconsistent, unreliable, or weak. It means you're human with a nervous system that responds to countless variables.

The practice isn't maintaining constant high capacity—that's impossible and exhausting. The practice is recognizing your actual capacity and adjusting your life accordingly.

This is the movement of Part Two: not forcing yourself to be different, but moving through life in ways that match your nervous system's current reality. With awareness, you can work with your capacity changes instead of being ambushed by them.

KEY TERMS TO REMEMBER

Window of Tolerance
The capacity zone where you can handle stress without overwhelm or shutdown. Changes daily.

Window Days
Days with expansive capacity for stress, socializing, and challenges.

Keyhole Days
Days with minimal capacity where everything feels overwhelming.

Capacity Debt
The natural depletion that follows high-capacity use, requiring recovery time.

* * *

Next: Chapter 5 Practice
Your gentle exploration of capacity changes

CHAPTER 5 PRACTICE

When Your Capacity Changes

Working with what you actually have today

* * *

Today's Capacity Check

Window Day ← **1 — 2 — 3 — 4 — 5** → **Keyhole Day**

Circle where you are today

Check what's true for you RIGHT NOW:

- ☐ Can handle noise vs. Need quiet

- ☐ Can be social vs. Need solitude

- ☐ Can focus vs. Can't concentrate

- ☐ Can help others vs. Need to protect energy

- ☐ Can make decisions vs. Decisions feel impossible

- ☐ Feel resilient vs. Feel fragile

Just notice. Your capacity today is information, not a grade.

Quick Reflection

My capacity today is affected by:

_____

What I need to honor about today's window:

_____

One thing I can cancel or simplify:

_____

I had to cancel three things yesterday. Felt guilty about each one. Then remembered: canceling when I have no capacity is self-care, not selfishness.

KEY TAKEAWAY

My capacity changes and that's normal.

Window days and keyhole days are both valid.

The practice isn't maintaining constant capacity— it's recognizing what I have today and honoring that.

Even when I can't honor it, just noticing is progress.

---

* * *

Next: Chapter 6 — When Anxiety Makes Sense
Sometimes your body is right to be alarmed

CHAPTER 6

When Anxiety Makes Sense

Sometimes your body is right to be alarmed

* * *

Your heart races before the meeting. Your stomach clenches when his name appears on your phone. Your body floods with adrenaline in the parking garage.

Part One taught you to observe these responses. Now comes the crucial movement question: Is your anxiety giving you accurate information that requires action, or is it phantom danger that needs soothing?

Different answers require different movements. Get it wrong, and you either ignore real threats or exhaust yourself fighting ghosts.

ANXIETY'S MIXED MESSAGES

My body says danger when he raises his voice—
but he's not my father.

My chest says run from this opportunity—
but is it threat or just visibility?

My stomach says no to this invitation—
but is it wisdom or just familiar fear?

Sometimes the alarm is accurate: this person isn't safe,
this job is depleting me,
this relationship needs boundaries.

Sometimes it's time-traveling: seeing dad in every authority,
mom in every criticism,
old danger in new faces.

Learning which anxiety to trust and which to thank but override—
this is the work of a lifetime.

The Evolution and Neuroscience of Anxiety

Anxiety evolved as our alarm system for survival. Your amygdala—the brain's alarm center—can trigger a full-body response in milliseconds, before conscious thought engages. This saved lives when threats were tigers. Now it responds just as intensely to angry emails.

Here's the crucial part: your amygdala can't distinguish between a saber-tooth tiger and your boss's criticism. Both trigger the same cascade of stress hormones, the same muscle tension, the same urge to fight, flee, or freeze.

Stephen Porges's research on neuroception shows that our nervous system unconsciously scans for safety or danger constantly. Some people's neuroception—often due to trauma or chronic stress—becomes calibrated to see threat everywhere. The body responds to perceived threat, not just actual threat.

This is why awareness matters: you need your prefrontal cortex (your thinking brain) to help assess whether the threat your amygdala detected is current or historical, real or perceived.

Connecting Anxiety to Capacity and Movement

Chapter 5 taught you to recognize capacity changes. Research shows that sleep deprivation and exhaustion directly affect threat detection. When depleted, your prefrontal cortex—which normally helps evaluate threats—goes offline. Everything feels dangerous because you've lost the ability to accurately assess.

The movement practice here builds on everything from Part One:

- Your observer (Ch 1) notices anxiety arising
- Your protector awareness (Ch 2) helps identify if this is protection or accurate warning
- Your body literacy (Ch 3) reads anxiety's physical messages
- Your neutral spot (Ch 4) gives you an anchor while assessing

Now you'll learn to move differently based on what kind of anxiety you're experiencing.

The Three-Step Pattern with Anxiety

1. NOTICE: "Anxiety is here. My chest is tight, thoughts racing about tomorrow's meeting with James."

2. VALIDATE: "This makes sense because..." (This step is crucial—it determines your movement response)

- "...James has actually been hostile lately" → Accurate anxiety
- "...authority figures trigger me since childhood" → Historical anxiety
- "...I'm depleted and everything feels threatening" → Capacity anxiety

3. ADJUST (different movements for different anxiety types):

- Accurate anxiety → Move toward protective action
- Historical anxiety → Move toward soothing and grounding
- Capacity anxiety → Move toward rest and restoration

When Anxiety Is Accurate Information

Sometimes your body is absolutely right to be alarmed. Research on intuition and "gut feelings" shows that our bodies often recognize patterns before our conscious minds do. This interoceptive awareness—your sense of internal body signals—can provide accurate information about threats.

Sometimes your body knows things your mind hasn't figured out yet.

That "off" feeling about someone might be your nervous system picking up micro-cues your conscious mind missed.

Accurate anxiety signals real threats like:

- A job that consistently violates your values
- A relationship where boundaries are repeatedly crossed
- A living situation that genuinely isn't safe
- Financial decisions that could harm your stability
- Someone repeatedly violating your boundaries
- Your capacity being exceeded (from Chapter 5)

Specific examples:

- Your presentation anxiety might be accurate (you're underprepared and the stakes are high) or historical (visibility always meant criticism in your family)
- That anxiety about your partner might be accurate (they're showing concerning behaviors) or historical (they forgot to text back and your abandonment wounds activated)
- The anxiety about your mom visiting might be accurate (she always criticizes your home) or capacity-based (you're too depleted for any visitors)

Body sensations of accurate anxiety:

- Often focused in the gut (hence "gut instinct")
- Specific to particular situations or people
- Consistent pattern over time
- Gets louder when ignored
- Often accompanied by clear thoughts about what's wrong

Kyle's Business Anxiety: An Illustration

Kyle was anxious about his business partnership with James. At first, he dismissed it: "I'm just scared of success again."

But when he used the three-step pattern:

Notice: "I'm anxious every time James messages me. My gut clenches specifically about him."

Validate: "This makes sense because James has shown three red flags: changed deal terms without discussion, missed two financial deadlines, and got defensive when I asked questions."

Adjust: "This isn't phantom anxiety. I need to act—get agreements in writing, set clear boundaries, maybe even reconsider the partnership."

Kyle's anxiety wasn't trauma response or success fear. His interoceptive system was accurately detecting that James wasn't trustworthy. The anxiety was trying to protect him from a real threat.

Cultural Context and Anxiety

How anxiety is understood and expressed varies dramatically across cultures:

Different cultural frameworks:

- In some East Asian cultures, anxiety might be described through physical symptoms ("my heart is troubled") rather than emotional terms, and this is the culturally normal expression

- Many Latin American cultures recognize "nervios" or "ataque de nervios" as legitimate conditions that blend anxiety with physical and spiritual elements

- Some Indigenous communities view anxiety as disconnection

from community or land rather than individual pathology

- In cultures emphasizing stoicism, anxiety might be seen as weakness to overcome rather than information to heed

- Some cultures see anxiety as a spiritual issue, others as purely biological, others as social

What this means for these practices:

- If your culture views anxiety as shameful, the "validation" step might feel wrong at first—that's okay, adapt it to what works for you

- If your family believes anxiety should be hidden or conquered, acknowledging it as information might feel revolutionary or uncomfortable

- Your "accurate" anxiety might include cultural stressors others don't face—discrimination, immigration stress, code-switching exhaustion

- Family might not understand why you're "paying attention" to anxiety instead of ignoring it

Important notes:

- There's no universally "right" way to relate to anxiety

- Your cultural context is part of your current reality, not something to overcome

- These practices can be adapted to fit your cultural values

- Sometimes anxiety IS an accurate response to cultural marginalization or systemic stressors

The Movement Response to Accurate Anxiety

Research shows that attempting to suppress accurate anxiety actually increases it. Your body knows something is wrong and will keep signaling louder until you listen. Fighting accurate anxiety is like unplugging a smoke alarm during a fire.

Clinical observations consistently show that anxiety about real threats needs different treatment than generalized anxiety. Real threats need real action.

Movement practices for accurate anxiety:

1. **Thank it first:** "Thank you, anxiety, for alerting me to this real issue.

2. **Take protective action:**
   - Set the boundary
   - Have the conversation
   - Make the change
   - Leave the situation
   - Get support

3. Discharge the energy after acting: Even accurate anxiety creates physical activation that needs release:

   - Shake it out (literally—shake your body like animals do after threat)
   - Walk around the block
   - Do ten jumping jacks
   - Take five deep breaths

The movement here is TOWARD action, not away from it.

When Anxiety Is Historical (Phantom Threat)

Your nervous system carries templates from past experiences. When current situations resemble past threats—even superficially—your body responds as if you're back there. This time-traveling anxiety is phantom threat.

Historical anxiety signals:

- Full-body activation (whole system responding, not just gut)
- Immediate intense response disproportionate to situation
- Familiar feeling you've had many times before
- Can't articulate specific current threat
- Pattern repeats across different situations

Movement practices for historical anxiety:

1. Acknowledge the time travel: "My body is remembering old danger."

2. Ground in present reality:

- Find your neutral spot (Chapter 4)
- Name five things you can see
- Feel your feet on the floor
- Remind yourself of current facts: "I'm 35, not 5. This is my boss, not my father."

3. Soothe the activation:

- Slow, gentle movement (not intense discharge)
- Warm bath or shower
- Gentle touch (hand on heart)
- Quiet, safe environment

The movement here is TOWARD soothing, not action.

When Anxiety Signals Depleted Capacity

Research on the window of tolerance (from trauma therapy) shows that when we're outside our window—either hyper-aroused or hypo-aroused—we lose the ability to accurately assess threats. Everything feels equally dangerous because our prefrontal cortex is offline.

Capacity anxiety signals:

- Diffuse overwhelm (everything feels threatening)
- Started after prolonged stress
- Worse when tired or hungry
- Can't prioritize actual threats
- Corresponds with keyhole days (Chapter 5)

Specific validation examples:

- "This makes sense because I haven't eaten in six hours"
- "This makes sense because I've been in crisis mode for three weeks"
- "This makes sense because it's 2 AM and I should be sleeping"

Movement practices for capacity anxiety:

1. **Recognize depletion:** "This anxiety is telling me I'm out of capacity."

2. **Rest before assessing:** Don't try to figure out if threats are real when depleted

3. **Gentle restoration movements:**
   - Slow walks (not intense exercise)
   - Restorative yoga
   - Gentle stretching

- Anything that rebuilds rather than depletes

Important: The Both/And Reality

You can have accurate anxiety AND handle it poorly. You can have phantom anxiety AND need to take it seriously. The categories help with response, not dismissal.

Kyle's anxiety about James was accurate AND intensified by historical patterns. The accuracy meant he needed to take action. The historical intensity meant he also needed to soothe his nervous system. Both were true.

Chronic Anxiety Is Different

Awareness can help both situational and chronic anxiety. But when anxiety is constant, awareness alone may not feel like enough. That's because the nervous system has learned to stay on high alert all the time. In these cases, awareness is still valuable, but it works best alongside other supports—like therapy, medical evaluation, or medication if needed. These practices as supplement, not replacement, for professional care.

Becoming an Anxiety Translator

When you learn to read anxiety accurately, you become skilled at transforming alarm into information, panic into practical action, or activation into appropriate soothing. You're not an anxiety alchemist turning lead into gold—you're a translator learning your body's language.

People with anxiety often have heightened interoceptive awareness— they feel every heartbeat, every sensation. This isn't bad—it's data that needs accurate interpretation. The key is learning which sensations signal real threat versus remembered threat versus depletion.

The Mixed Message Challenge

Often anxiety contains both accurate and historical information. Kyle's partnership anxiety had both:

- Accurate: James was showing real red flags

- Historical: Kyle's intensity came from his father's business betrayals

Movement practice for mixed anxiety:

1. **Separate the strands:** "Part of this is current (James's behavior), part is historical (dad's betrayal)."

2. **Validate both:** "It makes sense I'm worried about James AND that I'm extra activated because of history."

3. **Respond to both:**

   - Take practical action for current threat

   - Soothe the historical activation

   - Don't let historical intensity prevent current action

   - Don't let current threat trigger historical overwhelm

When You Can't Tell the Difference

Sometimes you genuinely can't tell if anxiety is accurate or phantom. When this happens:

The 24-hour practice:

1. Note the anxiety without acting
2. Care for your capacity (rest, eat, basic needs)
3. Find your neutral spot repeatedly

4. After 24 hours, reassess with a resourced prefrontal cortex

Often, accurate anxiety clarifies while phantom anxiety dissipates.

The trusted friend practice: Describe the situation to someone who knows your patterns:

- "Does this sound like a real concern or my old pattern?"
- "What would you do in this situation?"
- "What am I not seeing?"

* * *

Daily Practice with Anxiety

When anxiety arises today:

First, DON'T immediately try to calm it. Instead:

1. **Notice:** "Anxiety is here about _____. I feel it in my [gut/chest/whole body]."

2. **Validate with curiosity:** "This makes sense because... is it:

- Current threat needing action?
- Historical pattern needing soothing?
- Depletion needing rest?"

3. **Adjust with appropriate movement:**

- Current → Protective action
- Historical → Grounding and soothing
- Depletion → Rest and restoration

Remember This

Anxiety isn't your enemy. It's your body's alarm system that evolved to keep you safe. Sometimes the alarm signals real fire, sometimes it's reacting to burnt toast, sometimes the alarm itself is malfunctioning from exhaustion.

Your amygdala will always respond faster than your thinking brain—that's its job. But with practice, you can learn to quickly assess: Is this real threat or remembered threat? Is my neuroception accurate or miscalibrated? Am I resourced enough to tell the difference?

Learning to distinguish between these requires all your Part One awareness skills plus an understanding of how your nervous system works. The movement responses differ completely:

- Real fire needs evacuation (action)
- Burnt toast needs windows opened (soothing)
- Malfunction needs system repair (rest)

Don't make anxiety wrong for sounding. Learn what it's trying to tell you, then move accordingly.

KEY TERMS TO REMEMBER

Accurate Anxiety

Body's appropriate alarm about current, real threats requiring protective action. Often felt primarily in the gut.

Historical Anxiety

Body's time-traveling response, reacting to present with past programming. Often includes full-body activation.

Capacity Anxiety

Overwhelm signal that you're depleted and everything feels threatening. Diffuse, everything feels equally dangerous.

Neuroception

Your nervous system's unconscious assessment of safety or danger, which can be accurately calibrated or oversensitive.

Interoceptive Awareness

Your ability to sense internal body signals, which can provide accurate information about threats when interpreted correctly.

CHAPTER 6 PRACTICE

When Anxiety Makes Sense
Working with (not against) appropriate anxiety

* * *

Working with Anxiety as Information

Learn to distinguish what kind of anxiety you're experiencing and respond accordingly.

When Anxiety Arises

Step 1: NOTICE Where do I feel it in my body?:

    ☐ Gut (specific) → Often accurate

    ☐ Chest (tight) → Often emotional

    ☐ Whole body → Often historical or capacity

    ☐ Other: _____

What triggered it?: _____

Intensity level (1-10): _____

* * *

Step 2: VALIDATE WITH ASSESSMENT

"This anxiety makes sense because..."

Check all that apply:

- ☐ There's a real current threat (specify): _____

- ☐ This reminds me of past danger (what): _____

- ☐ I'm depleted/overwhelmed (Chapter 5 keyhole day)

- ☐ My values are being compromised

- ☐ Someone violated a boundary

- ☐ Situation genuinely isn't safe

- ☐ Haven't eaten in hours

- ☐ It's late and I should be sleeping

- ☐ I can't tell yet

Step 3: ADJUST WITH APPROPRIATE MOVEMENT

Based on your assessment, choose your movement:

If current threat → Take action:

- What boundary needs setting?: _____
- What needs to change?: _____
- What protective action will I take?: _____
- How will I discharge the energy after?: _____

If historical → Soothe and ground:

- Find neutral spot (Chapter 4)
- Remind myself: "I'm [current age], not [age when threat occurred]"
- "This is [current person], not [past person]"
- Gentle movement: walk, stretch, breathe
- What soothes me?: _____

If capacity → Rest and restore:

- What can I cancel/postpone?: _____
- How can I rest today?: _____
- What restoration do I need?: _____

If mixed (both accurate and historical):

- What part is current?: _____
- What part is historical?: _____
- Action for current part: _____
- Soothing for historical part: _____

24-Hour Reassessment If unsure, wait 24 hours then reassess:

- Day 1 assessment: _____
- Day 2 assessment: _____
- What changed?: _____

Weekly Pattern Recognition Track your anxiety patterns this week:

- How often was it accurate?: _____
- How often historical?: _____
- How often from depletion?: _____
- What patterns do I notice?: _____

Remember: Your body sometimes knows things your mind hasn't figured out yet. Listen, assess, then choose your movement accordingly.

KEY TAKEAWAY

Sometimes anxiety is accurate information.

Sometimes it's remembered danger.

Often it's both.

Acknowledgment calms my nervous system

more than any breathing exercise.

I can be anxious AND take action.

I can carry this feeling while doing what matters.

The goal isn't to eliminate anxiety.

It's to stop fighting reality.

---

* * *

Next: Chapter 7 — When Sleep Won't Come

Why your body won't power down when it doesn't feel safe

CHAPTER 7

When Sleep Won't Come

Why your body won't power down when it doesn't feel safe

* * *

Your night guard won't rest until it believes you're safe

It's 3 AM. You've tried everything—meditation apps, breathing exercises, counting backward from 1000. Your body is exhausted but your mind runs surveillance footage on repeat. Tomorrow will be hell, but knowing that only makes sleep feel more impossible.

What if the problem isn't that you can't sleep, but that part of you won't let you sleep? What if insomnia is your night guard, standing watch, refusing to let you become unconscious because it doesn't believe you're safe?

This chapter teaches you to work with your night guard through movement and dialogue, not fight against it.

THE NIGHT GUARD

3:47 AM. Neighbor's dog.
4:15 AM. First bird.
4:42 AM. Garbage truck two streets over.

I know every sound of dawn
because I meet it nightly,
wide awake despite exhaustion,
my body standing guard
for threats that retired years ago
but forgot to turn in their keys.

Perfect sleep hygiene:
Dark room. Cool temperature.
No screens. No caffeine.
White noise. Weighted blanket.
Meditation. Melatonin.

Everything right except the only thing that matters—
my body doesn't believe it's safe
to power down.

Why Sleep Is a Movement Practice

In Part Two, we're learning to move from awareness into response. Sleep requires the most profound movement of all: from vigilance to vulnerability, from control to surrender, from consciousness to letting go.

This isn't physical movement like exercise. It's the movement of your nervous system from protection to rest. Every night, you're asked to make this journey. When insomnia strikes, your system is refusing this movement because it doesn't feel safe enough to travel there.

The practice isn't forcing this movement but creating conditions where your nervous system feels safe enough to allow it. This connects to everything you've learned:

- Using your observer (Ch 1) to notice what's keeping you awake
- Understanding your protector (Ch 2) is trying to keep you safe
- Reading your body's signals (Ch 3) about what feels threatening
- Finding your neutral spot (Ch 4) as an anchor
- Recognizing if this is a keyhole day (Ch 5) with no capacity for sleep
- Assessing if anxiety is accurate or phantom (Ch 6)

My Mother's Night Guard: A Personal Discovery

For years after Kyle was born, I couldn't sleep. Not wouldn't—couldn't. My body refused to fully surrender to unconsciousness.

First, it was listening for the baby crying. Every sound jolted me awake. Was that him? Is he breathing? Even when he slept through the night, I didn't. My guard was on duty, monitoring his every breath.

As he grew older, the guard's job shifted but never ended. Now it listened for the door—was that Kyle coming home? Is he safe? Even when he was safely in bed, I'd lie awake, my body on alert for a crisis that might need me.

When Kyle became a teenager, my night guard went into overdrive. Friday nights were the worst. I'd lie in bed, one ear always listening for his car in the driveway. 2 AM, still awake. 3 AM, has something happened? Even after he texted "I'm safe, staying at friend's house," my body wouldn't believe it enough to sleep.

The revelation came during a conversation with my therapist:

"When did you become the night guard?" she asked.

"When Kyle was born."

"No," she said gently. "When did YOU first need to stay alert at night?"

And then I remembered: I was four when my father died. My mother, overwhelmed with grief, would cry at night. I'd lie awake listening, wondering if she was okay, if I should go to her. That's when my night guard was born—decades before Kyle arrived.

Having Kyle just gave my guard a new job. It transferred from protecting my mother to protecting my son. The guard had been on duty for over forty years.

Understanding Your Night Guard

Your night guard is the part of your nervous system that monitors for threats. During sleep, you're at your most vulnerable—unconscious, unable to respond to danger. If your nervous system doesn't believe it's safe to be that vulnerable, it won't let you fully sleep.

Clinical observations from trauma-informed practitioners consistently show that hypervigilance disrupts sleep. While we don't fully understand all the mechanisms, we know that people who've needed to stay alert for danger often struggle to fully surrender to sleep, even years after the danger has passed.

Stephen Porges's polyvagal theory offers one framework for understanding this: our nervous system needs to detect safety before it can move into states of rest. While this theory wasn't developed specifically for sleep, many clinicians find it helpful for understanding why some people's bodies resist the vulnerability of unconsciousness.

When your neuroception (unconscious threat detection) is constantly signaling danger, sleep becomes neurobiologically difficult. Your body is doing exactly what it learned to do to survive—staying alert. The challenge is when it keeps doing this long after the danger has passed. For some people, that danger was very real."

When Your Guard Is Protecting You from Real Past Danger

For people with PTSD or significant trauma history, the night guard isn't overreacting—it's responding to real danger you experienced. Your body learned that nighttime wasn't safe because it actually wasn't safe at some point.

This might apply if:

- You experienced trauma that occurred at night
- You needed to stay alert for real threats (abuse, violence, unsafe environments)
- Your trauma involved sleep vulnerability (assault while sleeping, nighttime raids, etc.)

- You were a caregiver who needed to monitor for actual emergencies
- You lived in genuinely dangerous conditions

Important considerations:

- Your guard's hypervigilance was an appropriate response to actual threat
- These patterns are deeper than everyday insomnia and need specialized support
- Dialogue practices might feel invalidating if they seem to minimize real danger you faced
- Your body might need more than validation—it might need evidence of current safety

Working with trauma-related sleep issues:

- Consider working with a trauma-informed therapist who understands sleep
- EMDR, CPT, or PE therapy specifically for PTSD might be needed before sleep improves
- Your guard might need to process the original danger before it can stand down
- Medication for PTSD-related sleep issues is often helpful and sometimes necessary
- Creating physical safety in your current environment is essential

Modified dialogue for trauma survivors: Instead of "You don't need to protect me anymore," try:

- "Thank you for keeping me alive when it wasn't safe"
- "I know you're trying to protect me from something that was real"
- "The danger you remember was real. Can we check if it's still here now?"
- "What would you need to see to believe we're safer now?"

Types of Night Guards

Different night guards need different approaches:

The Scanner (checking for threats)

- Constantly monitoring sounds, checking time, reviewing locks
- Learned when environment wasn't safe or when you were responsible for others' safety
- Often develops in new parents, caregivers, or those who experienced break-ins

The Replayer (reviewing the day)

- Loops conversations, analyzes interactions, reviews mistakes
- Processing incomplete experiences or social threats
- Common in people with social anxiety or perfectionism

The Rehearser (preparing for tomorrow)

- Planning conversations, imagining scenarios, preparing defenses
- Anticipating threats and trying to control outcomes
- Often develops during high-stress periods or major life transitions

The Processor (solving problems)

- Working through decisions, creating solutions, analyzing everything
- Trying to create safety through mental control
- Common in people with high responsibility or analytical minds

The Three-Step Pattern for Sleep

1. NOTICE (using Chapter 1 observer skills): "I'm awake at 2 AM. My mind is scanning for danger/replaying the day/rehearsing tomorrow. My body is tired but activated."

2. VALIDATE (the crucial Part Two addition): "This makes sense because..."

- "...my nervous system learned that nighttime required vigilance"
- "...when I was a new mother, being alert kept my baby safe"
- "...I'm genuinely stressed about tomorrow's presentation"
- "...my body doesn't believe it's safe to be unconscious"

3. ADJUST (movement toward rest):

- Thank the guard for its service
- Provide current reality update
- Use physical movements to signal safety
- Accept whatever level of rest is possible

Tonight's Simple Practice

If you only do one thing, try this:

1. When you can't sleep, say: "Thank you, guard, for trying to keep me safe"
2. Name one real reason you're actually safe right now
3. Touch your neutral spot from Chapter 4
4. Rest without forcing sleep

This alone can shift the dynamic from fighting to acknowledging.

The Dialogue Practice

Instead of fighting your night guard, try talking to it:

Basic dialogue structure:

You: "Thank you for trying to keep me safe. What are you worried about?"

Guard: [Listen for the answer—it might surprise you]

You: "That makes sense because [validate the concern]. Here's what's different now: [current reality]"

Guard: [Might argue or bring up new concerns]

You: "I understand. What would you need to feel safe enough to rest?"

My actual dialogue with my mother's guard:

Me: "What are you protecting?"

Guard: "The child. Always the child."

Me: "Which child? Kyle who's 31 and lives across town? Or the four-year-old me who was listening for her mother?"

Guard: "Both. All children need protection."

Me: "Kyle is an adult now. He has his own night guard. And that four-year-old? She survived. She doesn't need you to listen anymore."

Guard: "But what if they need you?"

Me: "If Kyle needs me, he'll call and the phone will wake me. If that four-year-old inside needs me, she can wake me from inside. You don't have to stay conscious to keep watch."

This dialogue continues to evolve. Some nights my guard believes me. Some nights it doesn't, especially when Kyle is traveling or stressed. But now I understand what it's protecting and can work with it rather than against it.

Movement Practices for Sleep

These physical movements help signal to your nervous system that it's safe to make the journey from vigilance to rest. Think of them as preparing your body for the movement into sleep, like stretching before exercise:

1. The Safety Inventory (for Scanners)

- **Why it works:** Physically confirming safety helps your guard stand down
- Walk through house confirming security (once, not repeatedly)
- Check loved ones are safe (one text, not twenty)
- Touch your neutral spot from Chapter 4
- Say out loud: "Everyone I love is safe right now"

2. The Discharge Shake (for Replayers)

- **Why it works:** Releases the day's activation from your muscles
- Stand beside your bed
- Gently shake your whole body for 30 seconds
- Let your jaw go loose
- Imagine shaking off the day's accumulated tension

3. The Progressive Settlement (for Rehearsers)

- **Why it works:** Gradually signals descent into rest
- Start standing, take three breaths
- Sit on bed edge, three more breaths
- Lie down, three breaths
- Each position moves you closer to sleep posture

4. The Butterfly Hug (for Processors)

- **Why it works:** Bilateral stimulation calms the nervous system (used in EMDR therapy)
- Cross arms over chest
- Alternately tap shoulders
- Continue for 1-2 minutes
- Helps integrate and calm mental processing

When Anxiety About Sleep Makes It Worse

Often, we develop anxiety about insomnia itself. "If I don't sleep, tomorrow will be ruined" becomes its own threat that keeps the night guard activated.

Using Chapter 6's framework:

- Is this accurate anxiety? (Yes, lack of sleep affects functioning)
- Is the threat immediate? (No, one bad night won't kill you)
- What movement helps? (Acceptance rather than fighting)

The Paradoxical Movement: Sometimes the movement toward sleep is accepting wakefulness:

- "I might not sleep tonight, and I'll survive"
- "I'll rest my body even if my mind stays active"
- "Lying here quietly is still restoration"

This removes the pressure that keeps your guard activated.

Real-World Sleep Challenges

These practices work alongside real-life factors:

- **Partners who snore or move:** Consider separate beds without shame—your guard can't rest with constant disruption
- **Children who need you:** Your guard might be accurately on duty—adjust expectations rather than fighting reality
- **Shift work:** Your guard is confused by irregular schedules—extra validation and patience needed
- **Perimenopause/hormones:** Physical changes affect sleep—work with medical providers alongside guard work
- **Chronic pain:** Address pain management while also dialoguing with guard
- **Caregiving responsibilities:** Your guard might have a real job—honor that while negotiating rest windows

The night guard dialogue doesn't replace addressing actual sleep disruptors.

Creating Safety Signals

Your nervous system needs consistent cues that it's safe to rest:

Physical environment movements:

- Arrange pillows as boundaries (your guard likes borders)
- Weight on body (heavy blanket signals grounding)
- Back against wall or headboard (no one can sneak up)
- Door positioned so you can see it (or closed for containment)
- Phone visible (so you know you won't miss emergency calls)

Ritual movements before bed:

- Check on loved ones once (satisfies scanner guard)
- Journal three sentences (satisfies processor guard)
- Gentle stretching sequence (discharges physical tension)
- Touch neutral spot while saying "I'm safe enough to rest"

When Nothing Works: Capacity and Sleep

Sometimes you can't sleep because you're in complete keyhole capacity (Chapter 5). Your nervous system is too depleted to do the work of down-regulating into sleep.

Signs this is capacity-related:

- "Tired but wired" feeling
- Been pushing through exhaustion for days/weeks
- Sleep gets worse the more exhausted you are
- Weekend "crash" sleeping after weekday insomnia

Movement practice for capacity-related insomnia:

- Stop trying to force sleep

- Focus on rest without sleep pressure

- Gentle restorative movements during the day

- Build capacity slowly

- Sleep will return as capacity rebuilds

When Professional Support Is Needed

This chapter focuses on hypervigilance-related insomnia. Seek professional help if:

- Insomnia persists beyond 3 months despite these practices

- You're using alcohol or substances to sleep

- Sleep issues are severely impacting daily functioning

- You have signs of sleep apnea (gasping, snoring, daytime exhaustion)

- Insomnia is accompanied by severe depression or anxiety

- You're having thoughts of self-harm from exhaustion

- Chronic insomnia is defined as sleep problems 3+ nights per week for 3+ months

These practices can complement but shouldn't replace medical evaluation for chronic insomnia.

Remember This

Your night guard isn't your enemy. It's the part of you that once kept you safe by staying vigilant. Maybe it helped you monitor a baby who needed you. Maybe it watched over someone you loved. Maybe it protected you from real danger. The guard developed for good reasons.

The movement from vigilance to sleep isn't about forcing your guard to abandon its post. It's about updating its information, validating its concerns, and gradually negotiating for rest.

Some nights your guard will stand down easily. Other nights—when loved ones are struggling, when the world feels dangerous, when old memories surface—it won't budge. Both are information about your nervous system's current state. Neither is failure.

Sleep is the ultimate trust fall. Every night, you're asked to fall backward into unconsciousness, trusting you'll be caught by morning. When that trust has been broken—by trauma, by responsibility, by loss—rebuilding it takes time.

* * *

KEY TERMS TO REMEMBER

Night Guard

The hypervigilant part of your nervous system that resists sleep to maintain safety monitoring.

Movement into Sleep

The nervous system journey from vigilance to vulnerability, from control to surrender.

Safety Signals

Environmental and ritual cues that tell your nervous system it's safe to rest.

Paradoxical Movement

Accepting wakefulness to reduce the pressure that perpetuates insomnia.

* * *

Next: Chapter 7 Practice
Your gentle exploration of working with your night guard

CHAPTER 7 PRACTICE

When Sleep Won't Come
Working with your night guard

* * *

Working with Your Night Guard

Learn what your guard needs to feel safe enough to allow sleep.

Identify Your Night Guard Type

Which sounds most like you at night?

☐ Scanner (checking for threats)

☐ Replayer (reviewing the day)

☐ Rehearser (preparing for tomorrow)

☐ Processor (solving problems)

* * *

Working with Your Night Guard

Learn what your guard needs to feel safe enough to allow sleep.

Identify Your Night Guard Type

Which sounds most like you at night?

☐ Scanner (checking for threats)

☐ Replayer (reviewing the day)

☐ Rehearser (preparing for tomorrow)

☐ Processor (solving problems)

The Three Steps for Tonight

Step 1: NOTICE

When I can't sleep, I'm:

- Thinking about: _____
- Feeling in my body: _____
- My guard seems worried about: _____

Step 2: VALIDATE

"This makes sense because..."

☐ There's a real issue to address

☐ Someone might need me

☐ I learned to stay alert for others

□ I'm too depleted to down-regulate □ My body learned nighttime wasn't safe

□ Other: _____

Step 3: ADJUST with Movement

Tonight I'll try:

- □ Safety inventory walk-through

- □ One check on loved ones (not multiple)

- □ Discharge shake before bed □ Progressive settlement into bed

- □ Butterfly hug for processing

- □ Dialogue with my guard

- □ Accept wakefulness without fighting

Dialogue Prep

Questions for my night guard:

1. "What are you protecting me from?"

2. "Who are you watching over?"

3. "What do you need to know to feel safe?"

4. "What would help you rest?"

Environmental Safety Signals

What helps my body feel safe:

- □ Door open / closed

- □ Phone visible / hidden

- □ Light on / complete darkness

□ Back to wall / open space

□ Covers tight / loose

□ Sound / silence

□ Other: _____

This Week's Sleep Pattern

Track what affects your guard:

- **Monday:** Slept? Y/N

- Guard worried about: _____

- **Tuesday:** Slept? Y/N

- Guard worried about: _____

- **Wednesday:** Slept? Y/N

- Guard worried about: _____

- **Thursday:** Slept? Y/N

- Guard worried about: _____

- **Friday:** Slept? Y/N

- Guard worried about: _____

* * *

Next: Chapter 8 — Movement as Medicine

Different nervous system states need different movement

CHAPTER 8

Movement as Medicine

Why your body needs different movement
on different days

* * *

Yesterday, running felt like freedom. Today, the thought of moving at all feels impossible. Last week, gentle yoga helped. This week, you need to punch something.

Part One taught you awareness—how to notice your patterns, read your body, find neutral zones. Now comes the culmination: using that awareness to recognize when movement will help versus harm, and adjusting accordingly.

This isn't about matching specific exercises to nervous system states. It's about recognizing when you're too depleted or too activated for certain types of movement, and having options that match your actual capacity.

THE BODY NAMES ITS MEDICINE

The exhausted body says:

I cannot move, I am empty, heavy as grief, still as stone.

Don't make me run— I'll shatter.

The activated body says:

I must move NOW, electricity in my veins,

if I don't discharge I'll explode.

The disconnected body says:

I'm here but not here,

floating outside myself— where did I go?

The regulated body says:

I can move or be still,

respond or rest— I have choice.

Learning when movement helps and when it harms—

this is medicine, not exercise.

The Truth About Exercise and Mental Health

Research consistently shows that exercise helps mental health—150 minutes per week of moderate activity benefits most people. But here's what the "just exercise" advice misses: **the same movement that helps when you're resourced can harm when you're depleted or overwhelmed.**

Studies show up to 50% of exercise's mental health benefits come from context and expectation, not just the physical movement itself. This means HOW you exercise—with friends versus alone, outdoors versus on a treadmill, by choice versus obligation—matters as much as WHAT exercise you do. Running with friends on a beautiful day because you want to hits differently than forcing yourself through a treadmill session because you "should."

Your awareness—built through Part One—helps you recognize these differences.

Using Awareness to Guide Movement

Everything you've learned leads to this moment of choosing:

- Your observer (Chapter 1) notices: "I feel heavy, can't get off the couch"
- Your protector awareness (Chapter 2) recognizes: "I'm shut down, not lazy"
- Your body literacy (Chapter 3) reads: "Shoulders collapsed, breathing shallow"
- Your neutral spot (Chapter 4) anchors: "Even exhausted, my earlobe is okay"
- Your capacity check (Chapter 5) confirms: "Definite keyhole day"
- Your anxiety assessment (Chapter 6) clarifies: "No real threat, just depletion"

All this awareness culminates in recognition: "I'm depleted. Intense exercise would harm, not help. I need gentle movement or rest."

Without Part One's awareness, you might force yourself to the gym, feel worse, and judge yourself for "failing." With awareness, you choose movement that actually serves your current state.

When Exercise Harms

Research clearly documents when exercise makes things worse:

Overtraining syndrome: Affects up to 10% of regular exercisers, causing depression, anxiety, and exhaustion. Your body literally can't recover between sessions.

Exercise-induced panic: For people with panic disorder, the physical sensations of exercise (racing heart, sweating, breathlessness) can trigger panic attacks. This requires graduated exposure with professional support, not pushing through.

Forced movement: Studies show mandatory exercise increases mental health problems. Choice matters profoundly.

Poor timing: High-intensity evening exercise disrupts sleep by delaying melatonin and raising body temperature.

When you're already depleted: Forcing intense exercise when your capacity is minimal (keyhole days from Chapter 5) deepens exhaustion rather than building resilience.

Recognizing Patterns (Not States)

Through observing many people (including myself and Kyle), I've noticed patterns in how bodies communicate their needs. These aren't scientific categories—they're practical observations that might help you recognize your own patterns:

Pattern: Depletion/Exhaustion

What I've observed:

- Body feels impossibly heavy

- Everything requires enormous effort

- Been pushing through exhaustion for days

- "Tired but wired" feeling

- Can barely find your neutral spot (Chapter 4)

What some people find helpful: Gentle walking, stretching, or complete rest without guilt. Sometimes the movement medicine is not moving at all.

Pattern: Activation/Overflow

What I've observed:

- Body vibrating with energy

- Can't sit still

- Racing thoughts

- Jaw clenching, muscle tension

- Feel like you'll explode without outlet

What some people find helpful: Vigorous movement that matches internal intensity—running, boxing, dancing hard. But note: for anxiety disorders, graduated exposure with smaller movements often works better than intense discharge. Work with a professional if you have diagnosed anxiety or panic disorder.

Pattern: Disconnection/Floating

What I've observed:

- Feeling outside your body

- World seems unreal

- Can't feel sensations clearly

- Going through motions automatically

What some people find helpful: Movements that enhance body awareness—pressing feet into floor, holding textured objects, swimming (feeling water boundaries). These are practical strategies people report helpful, though research on grounding techniques for dissociation remains limited.

Pattern: Balanced/Resourced

What I've observed:

- Can tune into body preferences

- Movement feels optional, not compulsive

- Can rest without guilt

- Body signals are clear

What's helpful: Whatever feels good. This is when standard exercise recommendations work perfectly. You might also use this time to gradually build capacity through progressive overload—carefully increasing intensity or duration to build resilience.

Kyle's Movement Mismatch: An Illustration

Kyle joined a CrossFit gym during intense work stress, believing high-intensity exercise would "cure" his anxiety.

"I was exhausted but wired," he told me. "I thought if I could just exhaust my body enough, my mind would calm down."

Three weeks in, he injured his back during a deadlift.

"Looking back, I was pushing through exhaustion and ignoring pain signals because I thought intense exercise would fix my stress. My body was telling me to rest, but I believed the 'no pain, no gain' mentality."

The injury forced complete rest for months.

"What I actually needed was to acknowledge my exhaustion first, maybe start with walking or gentle movement, then gradually build intensity as my capacity returned. Using exercise to override my body's signals backfired completely."

This illustrates why awareness matters more than following any rigid exercise formula.

The Three-Step Pattern for Movement

1. **NOTICE** your current patterns: "Am I exhausted? Activated? Disconnected? Or balanced with genuine choice?"

2. **VALIDATE** why this makes sense: "This pattern makes sense because [work stress/poor sleep/trauma trigger/keyhole day]"

3. **ADJUST** your movement accordingly: Remember: gradual progression usually works better than dramatic changes.

Movement Options (What Some People Find Helpful)

These are observations from clinical practice and personal experience, not prescriptions:

When exhausted/depleted, some people find helpful:
- Walking to the mailbox (tiny movement)
- Gentle stretching in bed
- Sitting outside (movement to fresh air)
- One yoga pose
- Permission to rest completely

When activated/overflowing, some people find helpful:
- Running or sprints (if physically safe)
- Punching bag or shadow boxing
- Vigorous dancing
- Cold shower (temperature change)
- Whole body shaking
- Note: Start small if you have anxiety disorders

When disconnected/floating, some people find helpful:
- Pressing feet firmly into ground
- Holding ice or textured objects

- Balance exercises

- Walking while counting steps

- Swimming (water provides boundaries)

- Any movement that enhances body awareness

When balanced/resourced:
- Whatever you enjoy

- Great time for progressive challenges

- Try new activities

- Social movement

- Or rest if that's what calls

The Role of Progressive Challenge

Even within these patterns, gradual progression matters. Research strongly supports progressive overload—gradually increasing challenge as your body adapts. This doesn't mean pushing through exhaustion, but rather:

- Starting where you are

- Adding small increments when ready

- Building capacity over time

- Respecting recovery needs

The key is progression should feel challenging but manageable, not overwhelming or depleting.

The Both/And Reality

You can know exercise helps AND be unable to do it. You can need movement desperately AND have no energy. You can do everything "right" AND still feel worse.

This isn't failure. It's information about your current capacity and needs.

Sometimes the movement medicine is admitting you can't move today. Sometimes it's moving despite not wanting to. Awareness helps you distinguish between can't and don't want to.

Creating Your Movement Toolkit

Based on what you've observed about yourself:

For depleted days:

- What's the smallest movement that counts?

  _____

- What gentle option feels doable? _____

- Permission statement: "Rest is medicine when depleted"

For activated days:

- What safe discharge works? _____

- Where can you do this? _____

- What duration helps without overwhelming? _____

  _____

For disconnected days:

- What helps you feel your body? _____

- What enhances body awareness? _____

- What movement has clear boundaries? _____

When to Seek Support

Consider professional help if:

- You have diagnosed panic disorder (need graduated exposure guidance)

- You have an eating disorder (exercise can become compulsive)

- You have chronic fatigue syndrome/ME (post-exertional malaise requires careful management)

- You're exercising compulsively despite injury

- Exercise consistently makes you feel worse

- You experience panic attacks during exercise

- You show signs of overtraining syndrome

- You can't tell if movement helps or harms

Remember This

The research is clear: standard exercise recommendations (150 minutes weekly of moderate activity) work for most people most of the time. Progressive overload—gradually increasing challenge—builds resilience. These proven approaches don't require complex analysis.

The patterns I've described (exhausted, activated, disconnected, balanced) are simply one way to think about when standard recommendations might not apply. They're observations from practice, not scientific categories. Your patterns might be completely different.

Your awareness—built throughout this book—helps you recognize when you're the exception to general guidelines. When forcing movement would harm. When rest is medicine. When gentle is better than intense. When gradual progression is smarter than dramatic change.

This chapter offers a framework, not the framework. Use what helps, ignore what doesn't. The only real rule is: pay attention to whether movement is helping or harming, then adjust accordingly.

Some days you'll guess wrong. You'll rest when movement would have helped, or push when rest was needed. This is the experiment of being human with a nervous system that fluctuates.

KEY TERMS TO REMEMBER

Movement as Medicine

Recognizing when and what type of movement will help versus harm, based on current capacity and needs.

Progressive Overload

Gradually increasing exercise challenge as your body adapts—the proven method for building resilience.

Context Effects

How you exercise (social, chosen, enjoyable) matters as much as what exercise you do for mental health benefits.

Exercise-Induced Panic

When physical sensations from exercise trigger panic attacks—requires graduated exposure, not pushing through.

---

* * *

Next: Chapter 8 Practice
Matching movement to your nervous system state

CHAPTER 8 PRACTICE

Movement as Medicine
Matching movement to your nervous system state

* * *

Choosing Movement Medicine

Use awareness to recognize when movement helps versus harms.

Current Pattern Recognition

Step 1: NOTICE Right now I observe:

- ☐ Exhaustion/depletion patterns

- ☐ Activation/overflow patterns

- ☐ Disconnection/floating patterns

- ☐ Balanced/resourced state

- ☐ Mixed: _____

- ☐ Something else entirely: _____

Body signals telling me this:

_____

Choosing Movement Medicine

Use awareness to recognize when movement helps versus harms.

Current Pattern Recognition

Step 1: NOTICE Right now I observe:

□ Exhaustion/depletion patterns

□ Activation/overflow patterns

□ Disconnection/floating patterns

□ Balanced/resourced state

□ Mixed: _____

□ Something else entirely: _____

Body signals telling me this:

_____

Step 2: VALIDATE "This makes sense because..."

□ Sleep quality: _____

□ Current stress: _____

□ Capacity level (Ch 5): _____

□ Recent events: _____

□ Other: _____

Step 3: ADJUST Based on my observations, movement that might help:

☐ Rest (movement isn't always the answer)

☐ Gentle walk

☐ Vigorous discharge (if safe)

☐ Body awareness movement

☐ Whatever I enjoy

☐ Progressive challenge

☐ Other: _____

Movement Experiment

Before movement:

- Energy (1-10): _____
- Mood (1-10): _____
- Body comfort (1-10): _____

After movement (or rest):

- Energy (1-10): _____
- Mood (1-10): _____
- Body comfort (1-10): _____

Did it help? _____

What did I learn? _____

Weekly Pattern Tracking

Observe what actually helps:

- Monday: Pattern___ → Movement___ → Result___
- Tuesday: Pattern___ → Movement___ → Result___
- Wednesday: Pattern___ → Movement___ → Result___
- Thursday: Pattern___ → Movement___ → Result___
- Friday: Pattern___ → Movement___ → Result___

What patterns do you notice?

_____

Building Your Personal Movement Guide

Through observation, I've noticed:

_____

When exhausted, what helps me:

_____

When activated, what helps me:

_____

When disconnected, what helps me:

_____

When balanced, I enjoy:

_____

Where I can add progressive challenge:

_____

Remember: 150 minutes of moderate exercise weekly benefits most people. But awareness helps you recognize when you need something different—or when you're ready for more challenge

* * *

Next: Part Two Conclusion
What you've learned about working with your patterns

PART TWO CONCLUSION

WHAT YOU'VE LEARNED ABOUT WORKING WITH YOUR PATTERNS

You began Part Two with a crucial question: "I can notice my patterns, but what do I actually DO about them?"

Now you have answers—not perfect solutions, but practical experiments based on awareness.

The Journey of Learning to Move

Part Two taught you a fundamental pattern that runs through everything:

Notice → Validate → Adjust.

This isn't just a technique—it's a different way of relating to your experience.

Chapter 5 showed you that capacity changes daily. You learned to recognize window versus keyhole days and, more importantly, to adjust your life accordingly rather than forcing yourself through. This wasn't about giving up but about working WITH your nervous system's reality.

Chapter 6 revealed that anxiety isn't always the enemy. Sometimes it's accurate information requiring action, sometimes it's historical requiring soothing, sometimes it's depletion requiring rest. The movement here was learning to respond differently based on what type of anxiety you're experiencing.

Chapter 7 introduced you to your night guard—the part that won't let you sleep because it doesn't believe you're safe. The movement was from fighting insomnia to dialoguing with it, from forcing sleep to creating conditions where rest becomes possible.

Chapter 8 brought everything together: using awareness to recognize when exercise helps versus harms. You learned that standard recommendations work for most people most of the time, but awareness tells you when you're the exception.

What Actually Changed

The shift from Part One to Part Two wasn't about adding techniques. It was about adding response to awareness.

Part One: "I notice I'm checking the locks again." Part Two: "I notice I'm checking the locks. This makes sense because I'm anxious about tomorrow. Let me acknowledge that anxiety and see if my hands can check just twice instead of five times."

Part One: "I'm having a panic attack." Part Two: "I'm having panic. Is this accurate anxiety about a real threat, or historical anxiety about a remembered threat? The response differs based on the answer."

The validation step—that middle piece—changed everything. Your body needs to be heard before it will consider changing.

What We Got Wrong (And Right)

Let's be honest: some of the frameworks in Part Two are more practical than scientific. The "window/keyhole" days, the night guard dialogue, the movement patterns in Chapter 8—these are useful ways to think about experiences, not proven scientific categories.

What IS scientifically supported:

- Capacity genuinely fluctuates based on sleep, stress, and resources
- Anxiety can be both helpful and harmful depending on context

- Sleep problems often involve hypervigilance
- Exercise helps most people but can harm when overdone or forced

What's practical observation:

- The specific categories and patterns described
- The idea that different states need different movements
- Some of the specific techniques suggested

Use what helps. Ignore what doesn't. These are tools, not truths.

A Day in the Life: Integration in Practice

Here's what using these tools actually looks like:

Morning: Sarah wakes exhausted after poor sleep.

Old pattern: Force herself to the gym because "exercise helps depression."

New pattern: Notice exhaustion (Ch 1), recognize it's a keyhole day (Ch 5), validate that rest is medicine when depleted (Ch 8), choose gentle stretching instead.

Afternoon: Anxiety rises about tomorrow's presentation.

Old pattern: Try to suppress it or catastrophize.

New pattern: Assess whether anxiety is accurate (Ch 6)—realizes she IS underprepared, takes action by spending an hour preparing, anxiety decreases.

Evening: Can't sleep, mind racing.

Old pattern: Take melatonin and scroll phone.

New pattern: Dialogue with night guard (Ch 7)—"What are you worried about?" Discovers it's afraid she'll forget something important. Writes tomorrow's tasks down, guard relaxes slightly.

Not perfect. Not fixed. But conscious.

Kyle's Integration

"I still have patterns," Kyle told me last week. "I still check things, still have migraines, still can't sleep sometimes. But it's different now."

"How?"

"I catch myself IN the pattern now, not after. Yesterday I noticed myself about to ghost James about a project. My protector was activated (Ch 2). But I recognized it, thanked it for trying to protect me, then sent a text saying I needed a day to think. Small adjustment, but I didn't disappear."

"And your body symptoms?"

"Still there. But I know the migraines often follow family calls where I don't speak up (Ch 3). So I'm practicing saying one true thing per call. Tiny movement toward honesty."

This is integration: not pattern elimination but conscious participation.

The Limits of These Approaches

These tools help but they don't:

- Cure mental illness (seek professional help)

- Replace medical treatment

- Work in crisis (crisis requires crisis intervention)

- Apply universally (your patterns might be completely different)

They're also not always accessible:

- Keyhole days might last months

- Some anxiety is too overwhelming to assess

- Sometimes you can't find a neutral spot

- Movement might be physically impossible

When the tools don't work, that's not failure—it's information that you need different or additional support.

Your Current Capacity

Acknowledge what you've built:

☐ I can sometimes notice patterns AND validate them

☐ I occasionally adjust based on capacity

☐ I've experimented with the three-step pattern

☐ I recognize when anxiety might be accurate

☐ I've tried dialoguing with resistance

☐ I notice when movement helps versus harms

☐ I'm learning when to rest versus push

If you checked even one box, you're doing the work.

The Bridge to Part Three

Part One gave you awareness—the ability to observe your patterns without drowning in them.

Part Two gave you movement—ways to respond to what you notice with validation and tiny adjustments.

But there's something else needed. Something about how we relate to others while doing this work. How we find and offer support. How we heal in connection rather than isolation.

Part Three will explore what I call "finding your others"—the people who get it, who share similar patterns, who can hold space for your work while doing their own.

Because while awareness is individual and movement is personal, healing happens in relationship.

Before You Continue

Take a moment to appreciate what you've built. You now have:

- The observer capacity to notice patterns
- The validation practice to acknowledge what makes sense
- The adjustment tools to experiment with change
- The wisdom to know when to rest versus push

These aren't small achievements. They're foundational skills that many people never develop.

Part Three will show you how to use these skills not just alone, but in connection with others who understand this journey.

PART TWO KEY PRINCIPLE

Awareness comes first.

Validation before regulation.

Tiny movements, not forcing.

Some days you can adjust.

Some days you can only notice.

Some days surviving is enough.

You'll forget this pattern.

You'll remember again.

That's the practice.

* * *

End of Part Two
When ready, continue to:

Part Three — Relationships as Practice
Or stay with these experiments longer. There's no rush

Imagine a rose and butterfly in love. When the butterfly flies away, the rose chases after it, dying in the process. This illustrates the importance of staying connected to our source, rather than prioritizing external things. JOY

PART THREE

RELATIONSHIPS AS PRACTICE

From inner awareness to outer relationships

You've built something real. Alone, you can notice patterns, validate them, make tiny adjustments. You've learned to work with your capacity, dialogue with your night guard, choose movement that matches your state.

Then your mother calls.

Three words in—not even critical, just that familiar tone—and every tool you've learned evaporates. Your carefully cultivated awareness? Gone. The three-step pattern? Forgotten. You're fourteen again, shoulders at your ears, defending against criticism that hasn't even come.

Or your partner walks in from work, and before they speak, your body is already matching their mood. Their bad day becomes your tight chest. By dinner, you're both   and neither knows why it started.

This isn't failure. This is the difference between practicing scales alone and playing in an orchestra. The skills are the same, but now you're navigating multiple nervous systems at once.

WHERE THE REAL PRACTICE BEGINS

Alone, I've mastered noticing.
Can catch anxiety rising, thank my night guard,
honor my capacity.

Then the phone rings.
Three words—not even critical— just that fa-
miliar tone, and my shoulders are at my ears.

That careful awareness? Gone.
The breathing practices? Forgotten.
I'm fourteen again, defending myself from criti-
cism that hasn't even come yet.

This is where the real practice begins— not
in the quiet of solitude but in the storm of
connection, where other nervous systems
crash into mine
and all my patterns wake at once.

Why Relationships Are Different

Part Two ended with a crucial recognition: healing happens in relationship. Now you'll discover why that's both true and terrifyingly difficult.

Your nervous system evolved to sync with others for survival. If one person in your ancient tribe sensed danger, everyone needed to activate quickly. "Oh, Bob's running? Maybe I should run too. Figure out why later."

This still happens through processes we're only beginning to understand:

- Mirror neurons that fire when you observe others' states
- Emotional contagion that spreads feelings like colds
- Unconscious calibration to others' nervous systems

You're not just managing your patterns anymore. You're swimming in a sea of other people's patterns, all affecting yours without anyone choosing it.

Last week I had beautiful morning awareness. Noticed my capacity (medium), thanked my night guard, matched movement to my state. Felt regulated. Centered.

Then my assistant called about a crisis with our biggest client. Within thirty seconds I was activated, defensive, heard myself saying "I'll handle everything personally!" My shoulders screamed "delegate!" while my mouth promised to take on everyone's responsibilities. Classic doormat response. All that morning awareness? Completely gone.

The Journey Through Part Three

Part Three explores what happens when awareness meets relationship, with each chapter building on the last:

Chapter 9: The Space Between Us

You'll discover why you're either a doormat or dynamite with boundaries. Your body learned these tools before you could speak, and they activate faster than thought. The automatic yes, the explosive no—there's another option, but finding it requires noticing which tool your body's reaching for.

Chapter 10: Bodies in the Same Room

This leads directly to understanding how nervous systems sync without permission. You literally catch emotions from others, matching their states before you realize it's happening. Learning when to sync and when to maintain your own center changes everything.

Chapter 11: The Relationship Mirror

When you understand syncing, you can recognize why that rage about the dishwasher is actually information. Strong reactions reveal where old wounds live. That 10% present trigger hits a 90% old wound, and suddenly you're furious about a spoon in the sink.

Chapter 12: Breaking Inherited Patterns

Those wounds often travel through generations. You hear your mother's words coming from your mouth. You're having your parents' fights with your partner. Three generations of "I love you, but..." stopping with you—if you can catch it happening.

Chapter 13: Living with Nervous System Awareness

Finally, you'll learn to live with all this awareness without drowning in it. Finding the middle path between hypervigilance about every pattern and unconscious repetition. How to notice when it matters and forget when you can.

What Makes This Advanced Practice

Relationships are where all your patterns show up at once. The checking pattern you thought you'd mastered? Your mother's voice brings it back instantly. The capacity awareness you developed? Gone the moment your partner gets stressed. The breathing techniques that work alone? Impossible when someone's crying in front of you.

Some people actually find it easier to maintain awareness with others than alone—if that's you, you might discover different challenges here. But for most of us, other people's nervous systems complicate everything we've learned.

Last month Kyle called: "I was doing so well. Then visited Dad for dinner. Every pattern I thought I'd worked through just... ran. Like I'd never done any of this work."

"The work isn't gone," I told him. "You just graduated to the advanced course. Now you're noticing inherited patterns, not just your own."

The Reality Check

You won't perfect this. No one does. But you'll start to notice the dance—sometimes even while you're dancing. And occasionally, just occasionally, you'll have enough awareness to choose a different step.

That moment of choice in relationship—when you catch yourself mid-pattern with another person present—that's where healing accelerates. Not because you handle it perfectly, but because you're finally working with patterns where they actually live: between nervous systems, not just within your own.

Ready to explore what happens when awareness meets relationship?

The real practice begins now.

The Space Between Us: Learning Your Body's Boundary Language

*Why you're either a doormat or dynamite
(and how to find the middle)*

THE TOOLS WE CARRY

Someone asks: Can you help me move this weekend?
My mouth says: "Of course, happy to."
My shoulders are already at my ears.

Three weeks of yes when I meant no.
Now Saturday at 5 a.m., I text:
"So sorry, throwing up, can't make it."
I'm not sick. Just hit my limit.

Or the opposite: someone disagrees
and I cut them off completely.
Delete number. Block on everything.
Burn the bridge with gasoline.

My body only knows two tools:
Doormat or dynamite.

But today—awareness first.
You ask for something.
I notice my shoulders rising.
I see which tool my body's reaching for.

"Let me think about it," I say.
Not forcing change, just noticing.
The awareness itself creates a pause.
A tiny space where choice might live.

Someone asks you for something. Before your brain even processes the request, your body reaches for a tool. The same tool it's used for years, maybe decades.

These aren't character flaws. They're survival tools your nervous system developed to keep you safe. The problem isn't the tools—it's that your body grabs them before awareness.

Last Tuesday, a friend asked me to water her plants for two weeks. "Of course!" my mouth said, while my jaw clenched so tight I thought I'd crack a tooth. By day three, I was furious—at her, at the plants, at myself. All because I couldn't notice which tool I was reaching for in time to choose differently.

Notice This Right Now

Okay, want to try something? Imagine someone asking you to help them move this weekend. Don't think about it—just notice your first body response.

Where does your body respond first? Shoulders? Stomach? Throat?

Does energy rise (ready to fight) or drop (collapse into yes)? Or do you go blank?

That response—whatever it is—formed before you had words. It kept you safe once. The question isn't how to eliminate it but: can you notice it before it runs you?

The Three Tools Your Body Knows

Think of these like tools in an emergency kit. When someone crosses a boundary or makes a request, your body automatically grabs one:

Tool #1: The Doormat

The automatic yes. You agree before thinking. Your mouth says "sure" while your shoulders tighten. You might have learned this tool if saying no meant losing love, facing anger, or being abandoned. Or it might come from cultural training about politeness, gender socialization about being accommodating, or family values about helping others. It kept you connected, even if it meant abandoning yourself.

Notice: When someone asks for something, do your shoulders rise while your mouth says yes?

Tool #2: The Dynamite

The explosive no. Anger rises instantly. You set boundaries like fortress walls— designed to hurt, to create maximum distance. You might have learned this if you had to fight for everything. Or you might have been socialized that anger is the only acceptable "strong" emotion. It kept you safe by keeping everyone far away.

Notice: Does heat flood your chest before you even understand the request?

Tool #3: The Disappearing Act

You go blank. Can't find yes or no. You leave your body entirely. You might have learned this if neither fighting nor agreeing kept you safe. For some people, this is trauma response. For others, it might be neurodivergent processing that needs more time. You survived by not being there at all, or you simply process decisions differently.

Notice: Do you suddenly feel far away, unable to access any response?

Important note: These patterns I'm describing—doormat, dynamite, disappearing—are simplified categories I've observed. Your boundary responses are likely more complex. You might be a doormat with family but dynamite at work. You might have healthy boundaries in some areas and struggle in others. Some people develop these patterns from trauma, others from neurodivergence like ADHD or autism that affects social processing, and still others from cultural training about how to behave. The patterns matter less than noticing what YOUR specific patterns are.

Why Your Body Grabs These Tools So Fast

Following our awareness-first principle: Before trying to change which tool you use, it helps to understand why your body reaches for it. Awareness of the mechanism creates space for choice.

Your Body Decides Before You Think

Here's what's wild: when someone asks you for something, your body has already started responding before you even understand the question.

Think of it like this—your body is like a really protective friend who jumps in front of you before checking if that's actually a snake or just a garden hose. By the time your thinking brain catches up, your shoulders are already at your ears or your jaw is already clenched.
This happens because the alarm part of your brain works faster than the thinking part. It's like having a smoke detector that goes off before you even see smoke.

The awareness practice: Notice your body's response happening. Just notice. "Oh, my shoulders are already rising." That noticing is everything.

The Social Context of Your Tools

Your boundary patterns weren't formed in a vacuum. Culture, gender socialization, and systems of power all shaped which tools felt available to you:

Women are often socialized toward doormat responses—be nice, don't make waves, keep everyone happy. Men are often pushed toward dynamite—be strong, don't back down, anger is the only acceptable emotion. Non-binary folks navigate both sets of expectations without a clear map.

Different cultures have vastly different norms about directness, conflict, and saying no. What looks like a boundary problem might be a cultural value about harmony or respect for authority.

Power dynamics matter too. Your doormat response with your boss might be practical survival, not a pattern to fix. Your inability to say no to your parents might be economic reality if you depend on them.

This doesn't mean you're stuck with these patterns, but it helps to recognize that some of them were adaptive responses to real external pressures, not just individual wounds.

Why You Developed Your Specific Tools

I learned this the hard way. My father died when I was four, and my mother raised me alone. Saying no to her felt like betrayal. Even now, forty years later, when someone needs something, my body immediately erases my own wants. The yes comes out before I can check if I actually want to do the thing.

Your boundary patterns developed at different developmental stages. Some formed before conscious memory—through thousands of tiny interactions about safety and connection. Others developed later through specific experiences you can remember. A harsh "adults are talking" at age five layers onto earlier, wordless learning about whether your needs matter.

If you're a doormat person:

When you were young, saying no might have meant someone got angry, withdrew love, or left. Or your culture taught that saying no was selfish. Your body learned: "Keep everyone happy = stay safe." Now when anyone asks for anything, your body immediately erases what you want.

Notice first: When someone asks for something, can you catch that moment when your needs disappear? Just noticing "I'm erasing myself" is the beginning of choice.

If you're a dynamite person:

You probably had to fight for things—attention, resources, respect, safety. Or you were taught that strength means never backing down. Your body learned: "Come out swinging = protect yourself." Now any request feels like someone trying to take something from you.

Notice first: Can you feel the heat rising before the explosion? That moment of recognition—"Here comes my anger"—that's where awareness lives.

If you're a disappearer:

Neither fighting nor giving in worked for you. Or you need more processing time than social situations allow. Your body learned the safest thing was to just... not be there. Now when someone needs an answer, you literally can't find one.

Notice first: The moment you start floating away—can you catch it? "I'm leaving my body now." The noticing itself can sometimes slow the leaving.

What We're Learning About Anger as Protection

Here's something therapists keep noticing: when people explode over small boundary crossings, there's usually something tender underneath that anger.

Last month, a friend asked to borrow money. I felt instant rage— completely disproportionate to the request. Later I realized the anger was protecting something else: my fear of being used, my sadness about past betrayals, my worry that saying no would end the friendship.

The anger was real. But it was standing guard over feelings I couldn't face in the moment. It's easier to be furious than to say "I'm scared you'll think I'm selfish" or "That hurt me" or "I feel unseen." Anger creates distance fast, keeps people from getting close enough to hurt the tender spots.

Important distinction: Sometimes anger IS the appropriate response and should be followed. If someone repeatedly violates your boundaries, if you're in an unsafe situation, if your rights are being trampled—that anger is trying to mobilize you toward necessary action. The question isn't whether anger is "right" or "wrong" but whether it's proportionate to the current situation or carrying old intensity. A good check: Would a neutral observer find this anger appropriate to this situation?

The awareness approach: When anger flares about boundaries, ask: "What is this anger protecting?" You don't need to fix it or change it. Just notice what's underneath. The noticing itself often softens things.

The exhaustion of using anger as your only boundary tool? It's like using a sledgehammer for everything. Need to hang a picture? Sledgehammer. Need to open a jar? Sledgehammer. Every boundary becomes a wall, every "no" becomes a declaration of war. You end up alone, surrounded by the rubble of relationships you destroyed trying to protect yourself.

I've been there—cutting people off completely rather than having one uncomfortable conversation about needs.

Your Body's Boundary Memory Bank

Your body keeps a record of every boundary experience you've had, even ones you don't consciously remember. When someone makes a request now, your body quickly checks those files and picks the tool that kept you safest before.

This happens faster than thought. That's why you might hear yourself saying yes while some part of you is screaming no—different memory systems are activated.

Awareness practice: After you've responded,138 notice: "Did my mouth and my body agree?" If not, that's information. Not failure—information about which memory system is running the show.

What Actually Happens: An Illustration

This pattern plays out constantly between Kyle and me. Here's a typical example with Maddy watching it unfold:

Maddy watches Kyle's shoulders rise before the phone even reaches his ear. His body already knows what's coming.

"I need you to drive me to the airport tomorrow. Five AM."

"Sure, of course—" The words tumble out while his jaw clenches.

Maddy catches his eye. "What's your body telling you?"

He looks confused. "What?"

"Your shoulders are at your ears. Your jaw is locked. What's that about?"

He pauses, phone still pressed to his ear. My voice continues, listing reasons why he has to help. But something shifts—he's noticing his body for the first time during one of these calls.

"Mom, let me check my schedule and call you back."

"Check what? It's a simple question."

"I'll call you in an hour."

This conversation changed everything for Kyle. Not because he suddenly could say no perfectly—he couldn't. But because he noticed his body's response while it was happening.

The Window Where Awareness Lives

Therapists talk about your "window of tolerance"—the zone where you can notice what's happening and make actual choices.

Inside the window: You can notice a request, notice your body's response, and choose. You have access to awareness.

Outside the window: Your survival tools take over automatically. No awareness, just reaction.

Here's the thing: you can't force yourself into the window. But noticing you're outside it—"I'm way outside my window right now"—that recognition itself is a form of awareness. Even noticing you can't choose is valuable information.

Trauma affects this window, but so does stress, bad sleep, hunger, and overwhelm. That's why on some days you can handle requests fine, and other days you're saying yes to everything or biting everyone's head off.

The Space Between Trigger and Tool

Viktor Frankl wrote: "Between stimulus and response there is a space. In that space is our power to choose our response."

The space between stimulus and response is always there, but trauma and stress affect how accessible it is. Think of it like a door that's always present but might be rusted shut, swinging too fast, or painted over. The door exists—that's the space Frankl described—but your access to it varies based on your history, current state, and the specific trigger. Awareness practice is like oiling the hinges, making the door easier to notice and eventually use.

When you notice your shoulders rising, you're seeing the space. When you feel your gut tighten, you're in the space. When you recognize "I'm about to say yes but my body says no," you've found the choice point.

I found mine last week. Friend asked me to help her move. Felt my shoulders rise. Noticed it. Also noticed heat building—that familiar anger starting to guard against feeling taken advantage of. But instead of exploding or vanishing into yes, I said, "Let me check my calendar and get back to you."

Revolutionary. Not because I said no—I actually said yes later. But because the awareness gave me a choice. I chose it instead of it choosing me.

Sometimes now, when I feel that familiar heat rising, I ask myself: "What is this anger protecting?" Usually there's something tender underneath—a need that isn't being met, a fear of being unseen, a sadness about how things are. Recognizing this doesn't make the anger wrong. It just helps me understand what's really happening. The anger is information, not instruction. It's telling me something needs attention, but it doesn't get to decide how I respond.

What Actually Seems to Help (Awareness-First Approaches)

Naming what's happening:

When you notice and name what tool you're reaching for—"Oh, there's my doormat tool"—something shifts in your brain. The thinking part comes back online just a tiny bit. The naming IS the intervention.

The two-second pause:

Not to force a different response, but to notice what's happening. "Someone asked. My body is responding. What tool am I reaching for?" Even if you use the same tool, you've now used it with awareness.

Noticing your body signals:

Before changing anything, just notice: shoulders rising, jaw clenching, stomach dropping. The noticing has to come first. Your body needs to know you see it before it will consider doing anything different.

Different Types of Boundaries

What we've been talking about—the doormat/dynamite pattern—is mainly about reactive boundaries. These are the split-second responses when someone asks something of you. But there's another kind: proactive boundaries.

Proactive boundaries are the ones you set in advance based on your values and what works for you.

Here's a real example: I don't want marijuana in my house, even though it's legal. This isn't about someone asking me in the moment and my body panicking with a yes or exploding with a no. This is a boundary I've thought through based on what I'm comfortable with in my space. When I communicate this, I'm not in doormat or dynamite mode. I'm just stating what works for me, from center.

Here's the difference:

Reactive Boundaries (this chapter's focus):

- Happen when someone makes a request
- Body responds before mind thinks
- Often tangled with fear of rejection or conflict
- The work: noticing your body's immediate response
- Example: "Can you help me move?" (shoulders rise, automatic yes)
- Example: "Can I borrow money?" (instant panic, either doormat yes or dynamite no)

Proactive Boundaries (equally important):

- Set in advance based on values/needs
- Come from conscious decision
- Easier to state from center (already decided)
- The work: standing firm when challenged
- Example: "I don't allow smoking in my house" (policy based on comfort)
- Example: "I don't lend money to friends" (decided in advance to protect relationships)
- Example: "No work calls after 7 PM" (protecting personal time)

Both types are about determining what you'll tolerate versus what you won't. What works for you versus what doesn't. But proactive boundaries bypass the doormat/dynamite pattern because you're not deciding under pressure. You've already decided from a calm, centered place.

The magic happens when reactive boundaries become proactive. When you notice patterns—"I always say yes to weekend requests and resent it"—you can create a policy: "I keep Sundays free." Now it's not a reactive decision but a proactive boundary you've141 already set. Someone asks you to do something Sunday, and instead of your shoulders rising while you panic-say yes, you can calmly say, "I keep Sundays free for myself."

When Honesty Isn't Safe

This chapter assumes you're in relationships where honesty about patterns is safe. That's not always true. If you're in an abusive relationship, at a toxic job, or dealing with someone who uses vulnerability against you, protecting yourself matters more than pattern work.

In unsafe relationships:

- Your 'doormat' might be keeping you safe from worse

- Your 'dynamite' might be the only boundary that works

- Disappearing might be the smartest option

Don't judge survival strategies used in genuinely dangerous situations. Get safe first, then work on patterns.

Building New Tools (Eventually)

You can't throw away your old tools. They kept you alive. But with awareness, you might sometimes choose different ones:

The Pause Tool

"Let me think about that and get back to you."

Buys you time to check in with yourself instead of responding automatically.

The Information Tool

"That doesn't work for me."

Not an attack, not a collapse. Just information about what works and what doesn't.

The Clarification Tool

"Help me understand what you need."

Gives you time to feel your actual response while gathering more information.

The Partial Tool

"I can do X but not Y."

Meets them partway without abandoning yourself completely.

These feel weird at first. Your body doesn't trust them. It's like trying to write with your non-dominant hand. But with practice, they become real options.

From Automatic to Conscious

Kyle called me back an hour later.

> Kyle: "I can't drive you tomorrow. Five AM is too early."
>
> Me: "What do you mean you can't? I need you!"
>
> Kyle: "I understand. But it doesn't work for me."
>
> Me: "You always do this. You're so selfish."
>
> (Kyle's shoulders rise. He notices. Breathes.)
>
> Kyle: "I need to go. We can talk later."

He hung up. His body was shaking. But for the first time, he'd said no from awareness rather than either automatic yes or explosive rage.

This is what progress actually looks like. Not perfect boundaries. Not calm responses. Just noticing your body's reaction and having a tiny moment of choice.

About That Fake Sick Text

Earlier I mentioned lying about being sick to get out of helping someone move. I'm not proud of lying. It reinforced my avoidance pattern and probably hurt my friend. What would have been better? Calling her when I first felt the 'yes' coming out wrong: "I just realized I overcommitted and can't help with the move. I'm sorry for the late notice." Harder to say, but it maintains integrity while honoring my limits.

Tonight's Experiment

Before bed, think about tomorrow. Is there something you've already agreed to that your body didn't want? Don't judge it. Don't try to fix it.

Just notice: "I said yes while my body said no."

That noticing—that gap between what happened and your awareness of it—that's where choice begins.

Tomorrow, when someone asks you for something, you might still say yes automatically. But maybe—just maybe—you'll notice your shoulders rising as the word comes out. And that noticing, even after the fact, is everything.

Preview Tomorrow's Boundary Moments:

What requests might you face tomorrow? _____

Which tool will your body probably reach for? _____

Can you commit to just noticing, not changing? _____

You're learning to hear what your body already knows.

Sometimes it takes practice to recognize the language.

When Professional Help Is Needed

If you recognize severe patterns here—never able to say no, exploding at everyone, dissociating constantly—please consider professional support. A therapist trained in somatic or attachment work can help you work with these patterns safely. Awareness alone isn't always enough, especially for patterns rooted in significant trauma.

Remember: Awareness First, Always

Everything described here comes from what therapists observe in clinical practice. But here's the key: none of these insights help unless you notice them happening in your own body.

You can't think your way to better boundaries. You can't force different tools. But you CAN notice:

- Which tool your body reaches for
- How fast it happens
- What it might be protecting
- When you're inside or outside your window

Your boundary tools developed for good reasons. They're not broken—they're just running on outdated information. But your body won't update that information until it knows you're paying attention.

The practice isn't to use different tools. The practice is to notice which tool you're reaching for.

Sometimes—not always, but sometimes—that noticing creates just enough pause for something different to happen. And when it doesn't? The noticing itself still matters. Your body is learning that you're watching, that you care, that you see what it's trying to protect.

That awareness is where all change begins.

Remember This

- Your body responds to requests before your mind evaluates them
- These patterns kept you safe once—they're not character flaws

- The space between trigger and response is always there, just moving fast

- Noticing your body's reaction creates possibility for choice

- Progress is noticing, not perfect boundaries

- Sometimes you'll still say yes when you mean no—that's okay

- Even noticing after the fact is valuable

- Reactive boundaries happen in the moment; proactive ones are set in advance

- Both types matter for determining what works for you

- Proactive boundaries bypass doormat/dynamite by deciding from center first

- Notice patterns in reactive boundaries to create proactive ones

- The anger is information, not instruction

- Awareness first, always

What I'm working on now: catching the signal earlier, before armor builds. Setting boundaries from center—calm, clear, kind—instead of waiting until I'm so resentful that my "no" comes out like an attack. The difference between "I can't do that" (from armor) and "That doesn't work for me" (from center) might seem small, but it changes everything.

Your body knows its boundaries. You're just learning to hear them. And honestly? Sometimes hearing them is enough, even when you can't honor them yet.

Key Terms to Remember

Doormat Response: Automatically saying yes to avoid conflict, disappointing others, or triggering abandonment.

Dynamite Response: Explosive boundaries that create maximum distance through anger or cutting people off.

The Space Between: The tiny pause between someone's request and your response—where choice lives if you can notice it.

Body Boundaries: The physical signals (shoulders rising, jaw clenching, stomach tightening) that show your true response before words come out.

Reactive Boundaries: Split-second responses when someone makes a request, often driven by body patterns from past experiences.

Proactive Boundaries: Boundaries set in advance based on values and needs, communicated from a centered, already-decided place.

Window of Tolerance: The zone where you can notice what's happening and have some choice about your response.

* * *

Next: Chapter 9 Practice

Your workbook for noticing body boundaries

CHAPTER 9 PRACTICE

The Space Between Us
Your workbook for noticing body boundaries

DOORMAT OR DYNAMITE CHECK-IN

Which tool does your body reach for?

Imagine this: Your coworker asks if you can cover their shift this weekend. Before they even finish the sentence, your shoulders are already at your ears and your mouth is saying "Sure!" Classic doormat move. You notice it happening—which is progress—but still can't stop it.

Then later, your partner suggests changing dinner plans. Small thing, right? But you feel heat flood your chest and hear yourself snap "Why do you always do this?" Boom. Dynamite. From doormat to explosion in one day. No middle ground, no calm "let me think about it." Just automatic reactions running the show.

Sound familiar? Let's figure out which tools your body reaches for.

Speaking It True - Doormat/Dynamite Edition

When your doormat tool activates:

Someone: "Can you help me move this weekend?"

Your mouth: "Of course, happy to!"

Your shoulders: "NOOOOO! We don't want to!"

You (noticing later): "I did it again. Said yes when everything in me said no."

Truth: "This pattern kept me safe once. Now it's just exhausting."

When your dynamite tool activates:

Someone: "Could you maybe—"

Your body: "RAGE. BOUNDARIES. FORTRESS WALLS. NOW."

You (after explosion): "That was... disproportionate."

Truth: "My anger is protecting something tender I can't look at yet."

* * *

Today's Body Boundary Tracking

Throughout today, notice which tool your body reaches for:

Morning request/interaction:

What happened: _____

My body grabbed: □ Doormat □ Dynamite □ Disappearing Act

I noticed: □ Before □ During □ After □ Not at all

Afternoon request/interaction:

What happened: _____

My body grabbed: □ Doormat □ Dynamite □ Disappearing Act

I noticed: □ Before □ During □ After □ Not at all

Evening request/interaction:

What happened: _____

My body grabbed: ☐ Doormat ☐ Dynamite ☐ Disappearing Act

I noticed: ☐ Before ☐ During ☐ After ☐ Not at all

* * *

Finding the Space Between

Remember Viktor Frankl's quote from the chapter? "Between stimulus and response there is a space." I'm still looking for mine most days. It's supposed to be where choice lives, but mine seems to be about a nanosecond long.

I'm always trying to find it. For example, recently when my friend asked to borrow money, I felt my whole body contract (doormat preparing) while anger rose (dynamite loading). For maybe half a second, I noticed both happening. That's the space! Then my mouth said "How much do you need?" while my jaw wanted to say "Absolutely not."

The space was there. I just couldn't use it yet. But I saw it. That counts for something.

> **The Space-Finding Experiment:**
>
> Next time someone asks you for something, try to notice:
>
> - The moment the request lands
> - Your body's first response (shoulders? stomach? jaw?)
> - The split second before words come out
> - That tiny gap—that's your space
>
> *Even if you can't use it yet, just noticing it exists is huge.*

What Your Body Already Knows

Your body has an instant opinion about every request. It knows before your brain catches up. Here's what I've learned mine does:

Body says NO signals:

- Shoulders climbing (protection mode)
- Stomach dropping (dread)
- Jaw clenching (biting back the no)
- Energy depleting (this will cost me)
- Slight backing away (creating distance)

Body says YES signals:

- Shoulders relaxed (no bracing)
- Leaning forward (moving toward)
- Energy rising (this feels possible)
- Chest open (not armoring)
- Breath flowing (not held)

Body says I'VE LEFT signals:

- Can't feel anything (numb)
- Watching from outside (floating)
- Can't find words (blank)
- Time feels weird (slow or fast)
- Can't access yes or no (gone)

Different Types of Boundaries

I just learned this distinction and it blew my mind. There are reactive boundaries (the doormat/dynamite stuff) and proactive boundaries (decisions you make in advance when you're calm).

Like, I have a proactive boundary: no work calls after 8 PM. I decided this from a centered place, not in reaction to someone calling. When someone asks to call at 9 PM, I can say "I don't take work calls after 8" without my shoulders hitting my ears or rage flooding my chest. It's already decided.

But when my mom used to ask me to drive her somewhere? That's reactive. No premade decision. My body has to figure it out in real-time, usually grabbing the doormat tool before I can think.

Proactive boundaries I already have (or want):

1. _____

2. _____

3. _____

Reactive situations where I struggle:

1. _____

2. _____

3. _____

Building New Tools (Slowly, Imperfectly)

The chapter talks about new tools we can develop. I'm trying to learn them. Key word: trying. Here's my reality check on each:

The Pause Tool

"Let me think about that and get back to you."

Success rate: 3 out of 10. Usually remember this exists about five minutes after saying yes.

The Information Tool

"That doesn't work for me."

Success rate: 1 out of 10. Said this once. Felt like a superhero. Haven't managed it since.

The Clarification Tool

"Help me understand what you need."

Success rate: 5 out of 10. This one's easier because it buys time while seeming helpful.

The Partial Tool

"I can do X but not Y."

Success rate: 4 out of 10. Compromise feels safer than full no.

Preview Tomorrow's Boundary Moments

This is brilliant and terrifying. Think about tomorrow. What requests might come? Which tool will your body probably grab?

Requests I might face tomorrow:

_____

Which tool my body will probably reach for:

_____

Can I commit to just noticing, not changing?

Yes □ I'll try □ That feels like too much pressure

What's Under the Anger?

This part of the chapter hit me hard. When I explode over small boundary crossings, the anger is usually protecting something tender. Last week I lost it when someone borrowed my pen without asking. A PEN.

Later I realized: the anger was protecting my fear of not mattering, of being invisible, of having my needs ignored. All that in a borrowed pen. The anger was real, but it was standing guard over old wounds.

When I notice anger about boundaries, I can ask:

"What is this anger protecting?"

"What tender feeling is underneath?"

"What am I afraid will happen if I'm not angry?"

Sometimes just asking reveals something. Sometimes it doesn't. Both are okay.

Tonight's Reflection

Today someone asked me for: _____

My body reached for: □ Doormat   □ Dynamite   □ Disappearing

I noticed: □ Before   □ During   □ After   □ Didn't notice

The space between trigger and response lasted:

_____

What my anger might have been protecting (if applicable):

_____

One tiny thing I noticed that I hadn't before:

_____

You're learning to hear what your body already knows. Sometimes it takes practice to recognize the language. Sometimes you'll notice the space but can't use it yet. Sometimes the old tools run completely. All of this is part of the process.

My body reaches for tools before I can think:
Doormat (automatic yes), Dynamite (explosive no), or
Disappearing (going blank).

These tools kept me safe once.
Now I'm learning to notice which one I'm reaching for.
Between someone's request and my response, there's a space.
Sometimes I can see it. Sometimes I can't.
Sometimes I notice it afterward.

The anger often protects something tender.
The doormat protects against abandonment.
The disappearing protects against overwhelm.

I don't need to fix these patterns.
I just need to notice them.
Even noticing after the fact is progress.

Listen, I wrote this whole practice section about boundaries, and guess what? While writing it, my neighbor knocked. Asked if I could pick up her mail while she's gone next week. My mouth said "Of course!" while my shoulders rose and my stomach sank. I NOTICED EVERYTHING and still said yes.

But here's the thing: I noticed. In real-time. I felt my shoulders rise, recognized the doormat tool activating, saw the space (couldn't use it, but saw it), and watched myself say yes anyway. That's actually huge. Six months ago, I wouldn't have noticed any of it.

We're not trying to have perfect boundaries overnight. We're trying to notice our patterns, understand our tools, and maybe—eventually—find that space where choice lives. Some days we'll use it. Most days we won't. That's okay. The noticing itself is rewiring things, even when the patterns still run.

Tomorrow I'll probably still be a doormat in the morning and dynamite by evening. But maybe I'll notice it happening. Maybe I'll see the space. Maybe I'll even use it once. Or maybe not. All of it counts as practice.

* * *

Next: Chapter 10 — Bodies in the Same Room

How nervous systems sync without permission (and why you leave family dinners exhausted even when "nothing happened")

CHAPTER 10

Bodies in the Same Room

How nervous systems sync without permission

EMOTIONAL WEATHER

You walk in anxious.
I don't notice at first—
then my breath gets shallow.
Within minutes my shoulders match yours,
both at our ears. We're syncing.

Or: I visit my depressed friend.
Leave feeling underwater.
Her collapse became mine
without either of us choosing.

But today: you arrive activated.
I notice my body starting to match—
breath quickening, tension rising.
I pause. Notice. Choose. Three deep breaths.
Feet on floor.

I don't abandon you,
but I don't join your storm.
My calm stays available
like a tuning fork—
here's the note,
find it when you can.

No rush.

Today's Focus:

Notice how bodies affect each other without anyone choosing it.

Your partner walks in from work. Before they speak, your breathing changes. Their shoulders are high and tight—now yours are too. Within minutes, you're both irritated and neither knows how it started.

Or your anxious friend visits. You were fine. Now, an hour later, you feel like you're drowning. Their worry became yours without either of you choosing it.

Or the opposite—you walk into your grandmother's kitchen and everything settles. She's not doing anything special. Just humming, making tea. But your body remembers: this is what safe feels like.

Bodies affect each other. You already know this, you just might not notice it happening.

Back in college, I had a perfect example of this. I was in my dorm room, feeling pretty good, actually getting through my psych reading for once. My roommate came home from what was clearly a terrible day—I could tell before she even spoke. Her shoulders were practically touching her ears, jaw clenched, moving through our tiny shared space like a thundercloud.

Twenty minutes later, I'm snapping at my laptop, shoulders tight, feeling inexplicably irritated about an assignment that five minutes ago seemed fine. It took me another hour to realize: I'd caught her mood. Like catching a cold, but emotional. I remember sitting there thinking, "Wait, I was fine before she got here. What happened?" That was my first real awareness of emotional contagion, though I didn't have a name for it yet.

The Science of Contagion (What We Actually Know)

Let me explain what research has established, while being clear about what's still being figured out.

Emotional contagion is real. Studies consistently show that people unconsciously mimic others' facial expressions, postures, and vocal tones. This mimicry then creates similar emotional states through what's called "facial feedback"—when you mirror someone's frown, it can actually make you feel sadder. But here's what's important: not everyone is equally susceptible. Some people are highly affected by others' emotions while some barely notice them.

Mirror neurons exist, but their role is complex. These specialized cells were first discovered in monkeys—they fire both when performing an action and when observing that action. While there's indirect evidence for mirror neurons in humans, scientists are still mapping exactly how they contribute to emotional contagion. What we do know is that something in our brains helps us unconsciously mimic others, though the exact mechanisms are still being studied.

Co-regulation is a developmental process. From birth, babies and caregivers regulate each other's nervous systems through interaction. A calm caregiver can soothe a distressed baby; an anxious caregiver may amplify the baby's distress. This continues throughout life—we affect and are affected by others' nervous system states. However, the degree varies enormously based on factors like:

- Individual sensitivity levels
- Attention patterns
- Neurodivergence (people with autism or ADHD may experience this differently)

- Cultural background (some cultures encourage emotional synchrony, others value emotional independence)

- Power dynamics (we're more affected by people who have power over us)

- Current capacity (when depleted, we're more susceptible to catching others' states)

Think of it this way: emotional contagion isn't like gravity—a universal force that affects everyone equally. It's more like sensitivity to temperature—some people immediately notice and respond to small changes, while others barely register them.

Important Clarification

When I say we "catch" emotions from others, I'm using a metaphor. It's not literally like viral transmission where exposure guarantees infection. It's more accurate to say we unconsciously tend to mirror others' states through various mechanisms—facial mimicry, breathing patterns, muscle tension—which can then influence our own emotional state. But this process is:

- Not inevitable

- Highly variable between individuals

- Sometimes under conscious control

- Influenced by many factors

Kyle and Maddy's Evening Dance

I watched this perfect demonstration last Tuesday when Kyle and Maddy came for dinner. Here's a typical example. Note that this is one way emotional contagion can happen—your experience might be completely different:

5:45 PM: Maddy arrives first, helping me cook, music playing. She's relaxed, laughing about something from work.

6:00 PM: Kyle walks in. I watch it happen—shoulders at ears, jaw tight, moving stiffly. Bad day written all over his body.

6:02 PM: Maddy, without even looking at him directly, turns the music down. Her shoulders start rising to match his.

6:05 PM: Both of them moving around my kitchen with the same tense, quick movements. The energy has completely shifted.

6:10 PM: Maddy snaps: "Why are you slamming cabinets?"

Kyle: "I'm not slamming anything! Why are you attacking me?"

Maddy: "I was fine until you got here!"

Kyle: "So it's my fault you're upset?"

Here's the thing—they're both right. Maddy WAS fine. Kyle WASN'T slamming cabinets (just moving with activation). But their bodies had synced to Kyle's stress state without either choosing it.

But—and this is important—not everyone would have responded like Maddy did. Some people might not have noticed Kyle's tension at all. Others might have noticed but not been affected. Still others might have deliberately chosen to maintain their own state.

The Before/During/After Practice

The next week, Maddy tried something different. She told me about it later. Note that this worked for her but might not work the same way for everyone:

What Maddy Did:

Before Kyle arrived: Quick body check. "Okay, I'm at baseline. Shoulders down, breathing easy, feeling pretty good."

When Kyle walked in: Noticed immediately. "His shoulders are high. He's activated. I can feel my body wanting to match."

Choice point: "I can feel my shoulders starting to rise. My breathing is getting shallow. Do I want to sync with this?"

Conscious decision: Three deep breaths. Felt her feet on floor. "I'll stay centered. My calm is here if he wants it, but I'm not joining the stress party."

Result: Kyle noticed her calm. Asked, "How are you so relaxed?" She said, "Good day. Want to tell me about yours?" He did. Talking helped. Her calm became the tuning fork instead of his stress.

She didn't abandon him in his stress. She just chose not to join it. This is advanced practice and doesn't always work. I tried this yesterday with my chronically anxious coworker. Worked for about five minutes before I found myself matching her breathing pattern again. But five minutes is better than zero minutes.

When Syncing Serves

Emotional contagion isn't always problematic. Sometimes it's exactly what's needed:

Appropriate syncing:

- Your friend is grieving. Matching their sadness (to a degree) says "you're not alone in this."

- Your child is excited about their drawing. Matching their joy amplifies it.

- Your partner needs validation. Matching their outrage about unfair treatment shows solidarity.

When to offer something different:

- Someone is panicking and needs calm presence

- A depressed friend needs gentle energy (not toxic positivity, just slightly more than they have)

- An angry person needs de-escalation

The key is developing enough awareness to sometimes choose whether to sync or offer something different. But remember: you won't always have this choice. Sometimes you'll sync automatically and only notice afterward.

Individual Differences in Emotional Contagion

Research shows enormous variation in how people experience emotional contagion:

Highly sensitive people (HSPs): About 20% of the population has heightened sensitivity to stimuli, including others' emotions. If you're an HSP, you might feel like an emotional sponge. This isn't a flaw—it's a neurological difference.

People with autism: May be less affected by emotional contagion in typical ways but might experience it differently—perhaps through anxiety about others' distress rather than directly "catching" the emotion.

People with ADHD: Might have difficulty filtering out others' emotional states, leading to either overwhelming contagion or, conversely, not noticing others' emotions when hyperfocused.

Cultural factors: Collectivist cultures often encourage emotional synchrony as a form of harmony. Individualist cultures may value maintaining separate emotional states. Neither is right or wrong.

Power dynamics: We're generally more likely to catch emotions from people with power over us (bosses, parents, teachers) than from peers or subordinates.

Protection Without Walls

You don't need to build walls to protect yourself from others' emotions. But awareness alone might not be enough, especially if you're highly sensitive. Here are strategies that some people find helpful:

For moderate sensitivity:

- Notice when you're syncing
- Take brief breaks (bathroom reset)
- Use grounding techniques (feet on floor)
- Name what's happening ("I'm matching your anxiety")

For high sensitivity:

- Limit exposure to highly dysregulated people when possible
- Schedule recovery time after intense interactions
- Consider whether certain relationships are sustainable
- Work with a therapist on boundaries if needed

Remember: If you're constantly exhausted by others' emotions, that's important information about your nervous system and might indicate a need for different strategies or support.

Reality Check: Positive Contagion

I've focused a lot on catching difficult emotions, but we also catch positive states. Your calm can be contagious. Your joy can spread. Your groundedness can offer others an anchor.

Some people are naturally good at maintaining positive states that others can "borrow." If you're one of these people, your regulated nervous system is genuinely a gift to others. But—and this is crucial— it's not your job to regulate everyone around you. That's exhausting and ultimately impossible.

Last week, my niece showed me a picture she drew and her whole body was vibrating with pride. I let myself catch it, matched her energy. We jumped around the kitchen together. It was perfect. Sometimes catching someone's emotion is exactly what connection looks like.

Some of my girlfriends are anxious. Like, professionally anxious. When I'm around them, I can literally feel my nervous system trying to match theirs within minutes. Now I know why I'm exhausted after every coffee date—it's not the conversation, it's the constant effort of trying not to sync with their activation level.

What Actually Helps (With Realistic Expectations)

Here's what I've found sometimes works, with the emphasis on SOMETIMES:

The Check-In Before They Arrive: Quick body scan. "Where am I starting from?" Just knowing your baseline helps you notice when it shifts. Success rate: When I remember, which is maybe 50% of the time.

The Feet on Floor Thing: When you feel yourself syncing, feel your feet. Literally. Sounds simple, works sometimes. "My feet are on the floor. I'm in my body, not theirs." Success rate: Varies wildly depending on how activated the other person is.

The Bathroom Reset: Excuse yourself. Go to bathroom. Shake it out. Three deep breaths. Splash cold water. Return. Success rate: Pretty good for mild contagion, less effective for intense emotions.

The Name It Game: "I'm noticing I'm matching your anxiety." Sometimes just saying it out loud breaks the spell. Sometimes it makes things weird. Use wisely. Success rate: Depends entirely on the relationship and situation.

The Reality Check

Look, I'm writing this chapter about conscious co-regulation, and you know what happened while I was writing it? A girlfriend called, stressed about mortgage rates going up. Twenty minutes later, I'm stress-eating cookies and worried about MY mortgage, which is locked in and totally fine.

We're human. We're wired to connect, and that includes catching each other's emotions. It's not a flaw—it's part of how we survived as a social species. The goal isn't to never sync. It's to notice when it's happening and occasionally—just occasionally—have a choice about it.

Some days you'll maintain your center while chaos swirls around you. Other days (most days for me), you'll catch every emotion in a five-mile radius and not realize it until bedtime. Both are normal.

Remember This

- Nervous systems sync automatically—it's not a choice initially
- Mirror neurons fire without permission
- You catch emotions like colds
- Sometimes syncing serves (grief, joy)
- Sometimes staying centered serves better (panic, anxiety)
- Noticing you're syncing is the first step to choosing
- You can offer your calm as a resource (when you have it)
- Some people will drain you—that's information
- Protection doesn't require walls, just awareness
- You'll still get pulled in sometimes—that's human

The truth? I catch everyone's everything. Always have. The person in line at the coffee shop having a bad day? I'll absorb it. The stressed parent at the playground? I'm suddenly worried about parenting (and I don't have children). The angry driver in traffic? I'm mad now too.

But now, sometimes, I notice it happening. "Oh, I'm syncing with their stress." Sometimes I can choose not to. Sometimes I can't but at least I know why I'm suddenly anxious about nothing.

That's the whole practice. Not perfection. Just awareness. Just occasionally having a choice. And being gentle with yourself when you don't.

Your calm is contagious too. Sometimes the greatest gift you can offer is your regulated nervous system. (When you can manage to keep it regulated, which is a work in progress for all of us.)

* * *

Next: Chapter 10 Practice

Your workbook for conscious co-regulation

CHAPTER 10 PRACTICE

Bodies in the Same Room
Your workbook for conscious co-regulation

Notice How You Sync Without Choosing

Okay, confession time. Many times, my friends call. They are sometimes stressed about work deadlines. Ten minutes into the call, I'm pacing around my office, shoulders tight, feeling stressed about MY deadlines which were completely manageable five minutes ago. I literally catch their stress!

You'd think knowing about emotional contagion would make me immune. Nope. I'm highly sensitive to others' emotions—what researchers call a "highly sensitive person" or HSP. About 20% of people are like this. The knowledge helps me notice it faster, but I still absorb a lot.

Important note: Not everyone experiences emotional contagion the same way. If you have autism, you might not sync with others' emotions in typical ways. If you have ADHD, you might hyperfocus and not notice others' states at all. If you're from a culture that values emotional harmony, NOT syncing might feel wrong. There's no universal "right" way to experience this.

Speaking It True

When someone's mood becomes yours:

Their anxiety: "Everything is urgent! Panic! Danger!"

Your body: "Starting to match... shoulders rising..."

You (noticing): "Oh wow, I'm syncing with their state. Do I want to? Usually I don't notice until it's too late, but hey, I'm noticing now!"

Truth: "I can stay centered and still be supportive. In theory. Sometimes. Okay, rarely, but it's possible."

When you offer calm (on the rare occasions you have it):

Your calm: "Here's a different frequency available."

Them: "Still activated but... noticing your calm."

Truth: "My regulated nervous system is a gift I can offer. When I can keep it regulated. Which is... a work in progress."

Simple Awareness Practice (Not Hypervigilance)

Instead of tracking every interaction (which could increase anxiety), try this gentler approach:

Once today, just once, notice if you caught someone's mood.

That's it. Not every interaction. Not constant monitoring. Just one moment of awareness.

When you notice it (if you notice it):

- What mood did you catch?
- From whom?
- How long before you realized?

This isn't about preventing syncing—sometimes syncing serves connection. It's about noticing it happens.

When Syncing Is Actually Good

Let's be clear: emotional syncing isn't always a problem. In intimate relationships, some syncing shows care and connection. Here's when syncing serves:

Healthy syncing:

- Your partner is excited about good news (join their joy!)

- Your child needs comfort (matching their distress briefly helps them feel understood)

- Your friend is grieving (some shared sadness says "you're not alone")

- Team celebration at work (shared positive emotions build bonds)

When to stay separate:

- Someone's panic that isn't based in current reality

- Chronic negativity that depletes you

- Anger that's disproportionate to the situation

- Others' anxiety about things outside anyone's control

The goal isn't to never sync. It's to notice when you're syncing and have some choice about whether it serves the moment.

People Who Affect Your State (With Nuance)

Instead of labeling people as "energy vampires" (which isn't fair or accurate), consider this reframe:

People/situations that often leave me depleted:

_____

(Note: They might be going through something difficult. This isn't about them being "bad," it's about recognizing your limits.)

People who help me feel grounded:

_____

People whose joy lifts me:

_____

Relationships where we co-regulate well (both give and receive):

_____

Important context: Someone who depletes you might be in crisis and need professional support, not avoidance. In work situations, you might need to interact with people who affect you strongly—that's information about needing recovery time, not permission to be unkind.

Practical Experiments (With Realistic Limits)

Here's what I try, with mixed results:

The Gentle Check-In: Once before a social interaction, briefly notice: "How am I feeling right now?" Not to create anxiety, just to have a baseline. Skip this if it makes you more worried about socializing.

The Feet Anchor: Feel your feet on the floor when you notice syncing. Works sometimes, especially with mild contagion. Won't work if someone is highly dysregulated or in crisis.

The Reset Break: If possible and appropriate, take a brief break. This assumes you can step away, which isn't always true. In meetings or family dinners, this might not be an option.

Spreading Positive States: When you're genuinely feeling good, notice if others catch it. Your calm or joy can be a gift—but it's not your job to regulate everyone.

When You're Highly Sensitive

If you're like me and absorb everything from everyone:

This isn't a flaw. It's a neurological difference. You process sensory and emotional information more deeply.

You might need:

- More recovery time after social interactions
- Smaller doses of highly activated people
- Regular alone time to reset your nervous system
- Boundaries that others might not need

And that's okay. Your sensitivity might also mean you're deeply empathetic, notice things others miss, and can offer profound support when resourced.

Cultural and Relationship Considerations

In some cultures: Emotional synchrony is valued as harmony. Not matching others' emotions might be seen as cold or disconnected. If this is your background, these practices might feel wrong. Trust your cultural wisdom about when syncing serves connection.

In intimate relationships: Some emotional syncing is healthy and necessary. If your partner never matched your emotions, you'd feel alone. The question isn't whether to sync, but whether you're syncing consciously or automatically.

At work: You might need to appear to sync with your boss's energy for professional reasons. That's not weakness—it's pragmatic. Just notice you're doing it and plan recovery time.

Tonight's Simple Reflection

Just one question:

Did I notice myself catching someone's emotion today? Yes / No / Not sure

If yes: What was it? _____

If no: That's fine. Awareness isn't constant.

If not sure: That counts as noticing something.

My regulated nervous system is a gift I can share. But it's not my job to regulate everyone around me. (Working on remembering both of these truths.)

Real talk: I absorb everyone's everything. Writing this practice section, I had to take three breaks—once because I could feel my neighbor's stress through the wall (thin walls, big feelings), once because reading about anxiety made me anxious, and once because... I forgot why. Probably caught someone's something.

But here's what's changing: I notice it now. Not always in the moment, but usually within an hour. "Oh, I'm angry. Wait, was I angry before Bob stopped by?" That noticing, even delayed, is progress.

We're not trying to become impermeable. We're trying to notice our permeability and occasionally have a choice about it. Some days we'll be emotional sponges. Other days we might manage to be slightly less absorbent sponges. Both are okay.

Tomorrow I'll probably sync with the first anxious person I meet. But maybe I'll notice it happening. Maybe I'll remember that their anxiety isn't mine. Maybe I'll even stay in my own nervous system for a full minute. Progress, not perfection.

* * *

Next: Chapter 11 — What Strong Reactions Tell You

When intensity reveals something about yourself
(and why you're furious about the dishwasher)

CHAPTER 11

The Relationship Mirror

What strong reactions show you

THE TEN PERCENT RULE

If the reaction fits the situation— ten percent
reaction to ten percent problem— that's just
life happening.

But when it's ninety percent reaction
to ten percent trigger?
When rage floods over dish placement?
When panic rises from a compliment?
When tears come from mild criticism?

That intensity isn't about now.
It's about then.
Your body is showing you
where old wounds live.

Today's Focus:

Notice when your reaction is way bigger than the moment warrants.

Your coworker is five minutes late. Again. Your body floods with rage— shoulders at ears, jaw clenched, heat rising. The reaction is way bigger than five minutes warrants.

Or someone compliments your work and you deflect, minimize, almost panic. "It was nothing, anyone could have done it." Your body rejects praise like poison.

Or your partner loads the dishwasher "wrong" and you're suddenly furious. Not annoyed—furious. Over plate placement.

The intensity might be information. Your body might be trying to tell you something. Or you might just be exhausted, hormonal, or legitimately frustrated about an ongoing pattern. Let's explore the different possibilities.

Last week, I completely lost it because Eric left a spoon in the sink. A SPOON. I went from zero to rage in about two seconds, launching into a whole speech about respect and consideration and how "this is symptomatic of bigger issues." He just looked at me, bewildered, holding this innocent spoon.

Later, after I calmed down (and apologized), I had to ask myself: What was that really about? Because it definitely wasn't just about the spoon.

A Framework for Understanding Intensity (Not a Rule)

Here's one way I think about emotional reactions—though this is my personal framework, not a scientific formula:

10% present trigger + 90% old wound = 100% overwhelming reaction

Sometimes your coworker being late (10%) activates old experiences of being dismissed, not mattering, being disrespected (90%). Your nervous system responds to all 100%. It doesn't know the difference between your coworker today and whoever made you feel invisible years ago.

But—and this is crucial—sometimes intense reactions have other explanations:

- You're exhausted and everything feels bigger

- Hormonal fluctuations are affecting emotional regulation

- You have ADHD or another condition that includes emotional dysregulation

- This is the fifteenth time this week someone has done this "small" thing

- The "small" thing is part of a larger pattern of disrespect

- You're from a culture that expresses emotions more intensely

- You're highly sensitive and experience everything more intensely

- Current life stress has depleted your capacity for minor frustrations

The 10/90 framework is just one lens, not the only explanation.

When Intensity Might Signal Old Patterns

Sometimes—not always—intense reactions do connect to past experiences. Here are some signs this might be happening:

Possible indicators of old wounds activating:

- The intensity surprises even you
- You have this same reaction repeatedly across different situations
- Your body responds before your mind understands why
- The feeling has a familiar quality you've felt many times before
- You can't quite articulate why you're THIS upset
- Later, you think "Why did I react so strongly?"

Kyle's Discovery: An Illustration

Kyle: "Emma left a cup on the counter. One cup. I lost it."

Me: "Lost it how?"

Kyle: "Yelling about respect, about chaos, about how one cup leads to total disaster."

Me: "Does this reaction feel familiar?"

Kyle: "..." Kyle: "You would flip when I was young. One thing out of place meant we were failures. Lazy. Would amount to nothing."

Me: "So Emma's cup might have..."

Kyle: "Activated thirty years of 'you're a failure if things aren't perfect.'"

Me: "Or you might just be stressed about work and the cup was the last straw?"

Kyle: "Actually... both. Work stress made me vulnerable, but the specific reaction—the 'failure' narrative—that's old."

When Intensity Is Completely Appropriate

Let's be clear: Sometimes strong reactions are entirely justified:

Your intensity might be spot-on when:

- Someone repeatedly violates clearly stated boundaries

- You're responding to actual disrespect or mistreatment

- This is part of an ongoing pattern you've already addressed

- You're dealing with systemic unfairness or discrimination

- Multiple "small" things have accumulated into a legitimate big thing

- Your body is accurately warning you about a real threat

Important: If someone regularly dismisses your reactions as "overreacting," that itself might be a problem. Women especially are often told they're overreacting when they're responding appropriately to real issues. Don't let this framework become another way to dismiss legitimate feelings.

The Body Connection (With Nuance)

Some therapeutic approaches suggest that intense emotional reactions often have somatic (body-based) components. While this isn't universal, you might find it helpful to explore:

When intensity floods:

- Notice: "Whoa, this reaction is bigger than expected."
- Locate it: Where in your body does it live? Chest? Throat? Belly?
- Get curious: "Is this feeling familiar?"
- Consider multiple explanations: "Is this old, current, or both?"

Note: Some people find this body-based approach helpful, others don't. If you have trauma or dissociation, this kind of body awareness might be overwhelming. Trust your own experience.

Emma's Praise Panic: Multiple Factors

My friend Emma couldn't receive compliments. Her body would literally contract. Here's how we explored the multiple factors involved:

"Your presentation was excellent," her boss said.

Immediately: shoulders forward, making herself smaller, words tumbling out—"It was nothing, Sarah helped, I just compiled things, anyone could have..."

Later, we explored several possibilities:

Cultural factor: Emma's family culture viewed accepting praise as arrogant

Gender factor: She'd been socialized that women should be modest

Past experience: Her sister struggled in school; praise for Emma meant tension at home

Neurodivergence: Emma has ADHD and rejection sensitive dysphoria—praise feels dangerous because it might be taken away

Current context: Her workplace is competitive; standing out feels risky

All of these factors contributed. It wasn't just "old wounds"—it was a complex mix of past, present, cultural, neurological, and situational factors.

Working with Intensity (Multiple Approaches)

Here are different ways to work with intense reactions:

First, validate the intensity:

- "This feeling is real and powerful."
- "My body is having a strong response."
- Don't immediately pathologize it as "overreaction"

Then, get curious about the source:

- Is this about something current that needs addressing?
- Is exhaustion/stress/hormones amplifying everything?
- Does this connect to past experiences?
- Is this my nervous system's baseline (HSP, ADHD)?
- Are multiple factors combining?

Avoid these traps:

- Using "it's old wounds" to dismiss current problems

- Endless analyzing that becomes rumination
- Ignoring real issues that need practical solutions
- Assuming every intense reaction means trauma

The Mixed Reality

Usually, intense reactions have multiple causes:

Kyle's rage about the cup contained:

- Current factor: Work stress lowered his capacity
- Past pattern: Perfectionism messaging from childhood
- Systemic factor: Pressure to be perfect at work
- Relationship factor: Emma had been leaving things out more lately
- Physical factor: He hadn't eaten in six hours

The movement practice for mixed causes:

- Acknowledge all factors: "I'm stressed AND this is touching something old AND I need to eat"
- Address what you can: Eat something, talk to Emma about the pattern, notice the old message
- Don't reduce complex reactions to simple explanations

Important Caveats

This framework doesn't apply when:

- You're dealing with actual abuse or manipulation
- Someone is gaslighting you about your reactions
- You have a medical condition affecting emotional regulation
- You're in crisis and need immediate support

Remember:

- Some people naturally have intense emotional responses—it's temperament, not pathology
- Cultural expressions of emotion vary widely
- Women's anger is often mislabeled as overreaction
- Current stressors can legitimately cause strong reactions
- Sometimes the dishes ARE the problem

When You Can't Tell the Difference

Sometimes you genuinely can't tell if your reaction is proportionate or not:

Try this:

- Give yourself 24 hours if possible
- Talk to a trusted friend who knows your patterns
- Consider all possible factors (current and past)
- Ask: "What would I tell a friend in this situation?"
- If unsure, address both current and past possibilities

The Reality Check

Knowing about this pattern doesn't stop intense reactions. I can write a whole chapter about the 10% rule (my framework, not science!) and still rage about spoons. Knowledge doesn't immediately change patterns that took years to form.

But it does help with the aftermath. Instead of spending days ashamed of my reaction, I can get curious. Instead of dismissing my rage as "just overreacting," I can explore what factors contributed. Sometimes it leads to insight, sometimes to practical changes, sometimes to both.

Remember This

- Strong reactions might signal old patterns, current problems, or both
- The 10%/90% framework is one lens, not the only explanation
- Intensity can be completely appropriate to current situations
- Multiple factors usually contribute to strong reactions
- Cultural, gender, and neurodivergent factors all matter
- Sometimes the "small" thing is actually part of a big pattern
- Curiosity works better than shame
- Don't use this framework to dismiss real problems
- Professional support helps when patterns are overwhelming

Three days ago, my friend was ten minutes late for coffee. TEN MINUTES. I was ready to end the friendship, delete their number, write them off completely. The rage was volcanic.

Later, I had to consider: Was this touching old feelings of being unimportant? Was I stressed about other things? Were they consistently late in a way that showed disrespect? Was I hungry? The answer: all of the above. The intensity had multiple sources—some old, some current, all real.

Be gentle with yourself when you have strong reactions. Be curious about what contributes to them. Consider multiple factors. And sometimes, just address the practical issue—maybe the dishes really do need a different system.

* * *

Next: Chapter 11 Practice
Your workbook for exploring intensity patterns

CHAPTER 11 PRACTICE

The Relationship Mirror
Your workbook for exploring intensity patterns

Quick Intensity Check

Which of these create outsized reactions in you? Check all that apply:

- ☐ Being interrupted
- ☐ Running late
- ☐ Receiving criticism
- ☐ Being controlled
- ☐ Mess/disorder
- ☐ Being ignored
- ☐ Authority figures
- ☐ Money topics
- ☐ Conflict
- ☐ Receiving praise
- ☐ Making mistakes
- ☐ Asking for help

Notice the patterns. What themes emerge from your checked items? Remember: having intense reactions doesn't mean something's wrong with you. People with ADHD often have emotional dysregulation. Highly sensitive people feel everything more intensely. Some cultures express emotions more strongly. Your intensity might be your normal.

Map Your Reaction (With Multiple Factors)

Think of a recent time you had a huge reaction to something small. Let's explore ALL the factors:

The trigger (what actually happened): _____

Your reaction (what you did/said/felt): _____

Where you felt it in your body: _____

Now consider ALL possible contributing factors:

Current factors:

- ☐ I was exhausted

- ☐ I was hungry

- ☐ Work/life stress was high

- ☐ This was the 10th time this happened

- ☐ Hormonal factors

- ☐ I was already overwhelmed

- ☐ Other: _____

Possible past connections:

☐ This reminds me of: _____

☐ I've felt this exact feeling before when: _____

☐ This touches an old worry about: _____

Systemic/relationship factors:

☐ This is part of an ongoing pattern of: _____

☐ There's a real issue here about: _____

☐ Power dynamics are involved: _____

Individual factors:

☐ I'm highly sensitive (HSP)

☐ I have ADHD/emotional dysregulation

☐ This is how my family/culture expresses emotion

☐ This is my temperament

☐ Other: _____

The reality: Your reaction probably had multiple causes. That's normal. It's usually not JUST old wounds or JUST current stress—it's a mix.

The 10/90 Framework (One Tool, Not THE Tool)

If you want to try my personal framework (not scientific fact!):

For your recent reaction: _____% present moment + _____% other factors = 100% your reaction

But remember: Sometimes it's 100% present and 0% past. Sometimes you're just legitimately pissed about the dishes because they've been left there every day for a month. That's valid too.

Important Reality Check

Before you go searching for old wounds in every reaction:

Is this reaction actually appropriate because:

☐ Someone repeatedly violates my boundaries?

☐ This is ongoing disrespect?

☐ I'm dealing with real unfairness?

☐ Multiple small things have accumulated?

☐ My body is accurately warning me about something?

Don't use the "old wounds" framework to:

- Dismiss your legitimate concerns
- Avoid addressing real problems
- Let someone gaslight you about your reactions
- Invalidate your own feelings

Sometimes your partner leaving dishes IS a problem that needs addressing, not analyzing.

Practice New Responses

When you notice a strong reaction, try these approaches:

- **The Validation First:** "Wow, I'm having a big reaction. That's okay. It's telling me something."

- **The Multiple Factor Check:** "What's contributing? Am I tired? Stressed? Is this touching something old? Is there a real current problem?"

- **The Both/And:** "This is partly about now AND partly about then. Both are real."

- **The Practical Solution:** "Regardless of why I'm upset, what needs to change here?"

- **The 24-Hour Rule:** "Let me sit with this and see how I feel tomorrow."

This Week's Experiment

Each day, notice ONE strong reaction (yours or someone else's) without immediately analyzing it:

Monday: What triggered it: _____

Tuesday: What triggered it: _____

Wednesday: What triggered it: _____

Thursday: What triggered it: _____

Friday: What triggered it: _____

At week's end, look back. Any patterns? Or just proof that life is legitimately frustrating sometimes?

When Someone Says You're Overreacting

This is important: People (especially women) are often told they're "overreacting" when they're reacting appropriately to real problems. If someone regularly dismisses your reactions:

Consider:

- Am I actually reacting to a pattern of behavior they won't acknowledge?
- Is this person invested in me being "wrong" about my feelings?
- Would they say this to a man having the same reaction?
- Is "you're overreacting" being used to avoid addressing the real issue?

Trust yourself. Sometimes the intensity is the appropriate response.

Cultural and Individual Differences

Remember:

- Some cultures express emotions more intensely—that's not overreacting, it's normal expression
- People with ADHD often have rejection sensitive dysphoria—intense emotional responses to perceived rejection
- HSPs (highly sensitive people) feel everything more deeply—it's neurological, not drama
- Neurodivergent people might have different emotional regulation—it's difference, not deficit
- Your normal might be someone else's "too much" and that's okay

When to Seek Support

Consider professional help if:

- Every small thing triggers huge reactions
- You can't recover from emotional intensity
- Your reactions are damaging relationships
- You feel constantly triggered
- You can't tell if your reactions are proportionate

This isn't weakness—it's recognizing when patterns need more support than self-help can provide.

Tonight's Reflection

Today's strongest reaction was to: _____

Contributing factors I can identify:

Current: _____

Possible past: _____

Physical (tired/hungry): _____

Systemic/ongoing: _____

Whatthisreactionmightbetryingtotellme:_____

One practical thing I could change: _____

KEY TAKEAWAY

Strong reactions usually have multiple causes. The 10/90 framework is one lens, not the only truth. Sometimes intensity is completely appropriate. Current stress matters as much as old patterns. Different people have different emotional baselines. Curiosity beats shame every time.

Don't let "working on yourself" become a way to avoid addressing real problems in your relationships or life.

Remember: Your intense reaction to the dishes might be about childhood messages about perfection. OR it might be about your partner consistently not doing their share. OR you might be exhausted. OR you have ADHD and transitions are hard. OR all of the above.

The point isn't to find THE answer but to be curious about all the factors. And sometimes, the most important thing isn't understanding why you're upset—it's addressing what needs to change.

Be gentle with your intensity. Be curious about it. But also trust it—sometimes it's telling you something important about what needs to be different in your life right now, not what happened in your past.

* * *

Next: Chapter 12
Breaking Inherited Patterns

CHAPTER 12

Breaking Inherited Patterns

*How generational trauma shows up
in your relationships*

THE INHERITANCE

From mother: how to scan for danger, shoulders

always slightly raised.

How to say "I'm fine" through anything. How to

give until empty, then give more.

From father: how to leave the room when

feelings get too big.

How silence can be a weapon.

How work matters more than presence.

From grandmother: how to survive

by making yourself smaller.

How to smile when you're dying inside.
How to never, ever ask for help.

From absence: how to imagine

what was never modeled.

These patterns lived in their bodies first, now

they live in mine.

But I can choose

which ones die with me.

Your partner asks why you can't just say "I love you" without adding "but." You don't know. The words get stuck. Then you remember: your mother never said it without conditions. Your father's love came with performance reviews. Three generations of "I love you, but you could do better."

Or you're having a normal disagreement with your spouse when suddenly you're your father—jaw set, walking away, silent treatment deployed. Your partner becomes your mother in that moment, and you're both recreating a 30-year-old fight that isn't even yours.

Or you watch yourself pushing your children away right when they need you most, and realize—this is exactly what your parent did. The pattern you swore you'd never repeat, now playing out in your own relationships.

You don't just inherit eye color. You inherit relationship blueprints. But here's what's crucial to understand: these patterns are transmitted through multiple pathways—genetics, learned behavior, environmental factors, and sometimes all three. Let's explore how this actually works.

How Relationship Patterns Travel (It's Complicated)

Before we dive into how patterns are passed down, let's be clear: correlation doesn't equal causation. If you're anxious like your mother, it could be because:

- You inherited genetic variants associated with anxiety
- You learned anxious responses by observing her

- You both respond to similar environmental stressors
- Some combination of all these factors
- Or it could be coincidence

Research suggests all these pathways contribute:

Genetic factors: Studies show that anxiety, depression, and attachment styles have heritable components—ranging from 30-50% depending on the trait. This means genetics plays a role, but it's not destiny.

Behavioral modeling: Through thousands of daily interactions, children observe and internalize relationship patterns. Mirror neurons may play a role in this learning, though the exact mechanisms in humans are still being mapped.

Co-regulation: A parent's regulated or dysregulated nervous system affects their child's developing nervous system. This is well-established. But remember—children aren't passive recipients. They actively interpret and sometimes reject what they observe.

Environmental factors: Families often face similar stressors across generations—poverty, discrimination, migration. Similar patterns might emerge as adaptive responses to similar challenges, not necessarily direct transmission.

What this means: You're not doomed to repeat your parents' patterns, but you might have tendencies—both genetic and learned—that lean you in certain directions. Awareness helps you choose which tendencies to follow and which to redirect.

Three Generations in One Room

Kyle called me over last week. He's been thinking about having kids with Maddy, and he's terrified of passing on what I passed to him. We sat talking about what might happen, what he fears, what patterns he's already noticed rising in his relationship.

Kyle: "What if I tell my kid to stop crying, like you used to tell me? What if those words just... come out?"

Me: "They probably will. The words rose in my throat every time you cried. Still do sometimes when I see anyone crying."

Kyle: "So I'm doomed to repeat it?"

Me: "No. You'll feel the words rising. Your shoulders will go up, your jaw will get tight—just like mine did, just like my mother's did. But you'll notice. And in that noticing, you'll have a choice."

Kyle: "How do you know?"

Me: "Because you're already noticing it with Maddy. Last week when she was upset, you started to say 'you're being too sensitive'—my exact words—but you caught yourself."

Kyle: "I heard your voice. Actually, I heard Grandma's voice coming through yours coming through mine."

Me: "Three generations in one sentence. But you caught it. That's the difference. That's what breaks the pattern."

Kyle: *"What if I don't catch it in time with my kids?"*

Me: *"Then you repair it. You say, 'That wasn't kind. Daddy said something his mommy used to say, and it wasn't right. Your feelings matter.' The repair might be more powerful than never messing up at all."*

The Reality of Pattern Transmission

Let's look at what research actually tells us about how patterns are passed down:

Attachment patterns: Research shows about 70% correspondence between parent and child attachment styles. But that means 30% of children develop different attachment styles than their parents. Plus, people can develop "earned secure attachment" through healing relationships, even if they didn't receive it in childhood.

Implicit learning: Before conscious memory forms (around age 2-3), children are absorbing patterns through repeated interactions. But these aren't fixed programs—they're tendencies that can be modified throughout life.

Neuroplasticity: Your brain remains capable of forming new patterns throughout your entire life. Each time you notice an inherited pattern and choose differently, you're literally creating new neural pathways.

Important caveat: Not all automatic responses are childhood implicit memories. Some are just habits, preferences, or responses to current situations. Don't assume every pattern has deep roots.

What You Might Have Inherited (Nature AND Nurture)

Different parenting styles tend to create certain patterns, but remember—these are tendencies, not destinies. Plus, genetics and temperament play huge roles:

From anxious parents:

- Genetic predisposition to anxiety (heritable component: ~30-40%)
- Learned hypervigilance and worry patterns
- But also possibly: inherited resilience, problem-solving skills, empathy

From avoidant parents:

- Possible genetic factors affecting emotional expression
- Learned patterns of emotional distance
- But also possibly: independence, self-reliance, calm in crisis

From inconsistent parents:

- Confusion about what to expect in relationships
- But also possibly: adaptability, reading people well, flexibility

Remember sibling differences: Children from the same family often develop completely different patterns because:

- Each child has unique genetic combinations
- Birth order affects experience
- Each child interprets family dynamics differently
- Peer relationships shape patterns too

- Individual temperament influences how patterns are received

Inherited Strengths (Not Just Wounds)

We focus so much on inherited trauma that we forget inherited resilience:

What else you might have inherited:

- Your grandmother's ability to laugh during hard times
- Your father's persistence through challenges
- Your mother's creativity in making something from nothing
- Your grandfather's way of showing love through actions
- Family humor that helps cope with difficulty
- Cultural wisdom about surviving and thriving
- Ways of staying connected despite conflict

Kyle realized this last week: "I inherited your anxiety, but I also inherited your determination to understand it. That's a gift too."

The Interrupt in Relationships

You can't delete inherited patterns, but you can interrupt them—right in the middle of your interactions. Here's what I've learned:

When the pattern runs with your partner:

You hear yourself using your mother's guilt tactics. The interrupt: "Wait, that's my mom's voice. That's not fair to you. Let me try again."

You're stonewalling like your father. The interrupt: "I'm shutting down like my dad did. Give me five minutes to come back to you."

You're recreating your parents' dynamic. The interrupt: "We're having my parents' fight right now. Can we pause and remember we're us?"

The key: These interrupts work because you're acknowledging both the pattern AND your agency to choose differently.

Breaking Patterns for the Next Generation

Kyle called me yesterday with a realization:

Kyle: "My godson was crying at dinner. His mom told him to stop, that boys don't cry."

Me: "What did you notice in yourself?"

Kyle: "The words 'she's right' were right there in my throat. I felt them rising. My whole body agreed with her."

Me: "But?"

Kyle: "But I noticed them. Took a breath. Told the kid, 'It's okay to cry when you're sad. That's what tears are for.'"

Me: "You just practiced for your future children. You interrupted a pattern before you even have kids to pass it to."

This is how patterns break—not through perfection, but through catching them and choosing differently, one interaction at a time.

Individual Agency and Choice

Here's what often gets lost in discussions of inherited patterns: You're not a passive recipient. You're actively choosing—consciously or unconsciously—which patterns to keep, modify, or reject.

Factors that influence pattern breaking:

- Education and awareness (like reading this book)
- Different life experiences than your parents
- Therapy or healing relationships
- Peer and partner influences
- Cultural changes between generations
- Your own unique temperament and interpretations
- Sometimes, sheer determination

The Compassion Part

Your parents gave you their patterns because that's what they had to give. They inherited them too—through genetics, modeling, and their own experiences.

But understanding this doesn't mean you're stuck. It means you can have compassion for the source while still choosing differently. They couldn't teach you what they never learned, but you can learn it now.

When Professional Support Helps

Consider therapy for inherited patterns when:

- You keep recreating dynamics you hate

- You can't interrupt patterns even when you notice them
- Inherited trauma significantly impacts your relationships
- You're afraid to have children because of what you might pass on
- You need help building earned secure attachment

Remember: therapists can help you sort out what's genetic, what's learned, what's current, and what you want to change.

Remember This

- Patterns are transmitted through genetics, behavior, and environment—usually all three
- Correlation doesn't equal causation—similar patterns might have different sources
- 70% attachment correspondence means 30% develop different patterns
- Siblings often have completely different patterns despite same parents
- You inherit strengths and resilience, not just wounds
- Children actively interpret patterns, not passively receive them
- Neuroplasticity means change is possible throughout life
- Earned secure attachment is achievable
- Professional support can help sort complex inheritance
- You have agency in choosing which patterns continue

One day, Kyle's children will tell him, "Daddy, you're different than other daddies. You let me feel things." They'll grow up knowing feelings are allowed, that repair is possible, that love doesn't require perfection.

That's the power of awareness—it doesn't just change you, it changes every relationship that will come.

The patterns will still rise. Your mother's voice will still emerge. Your genetic tendencies will still be there. But now you notice. And in that noticing, there's a moment—just a moment—where you can choose.

That moment changes everything.

* * *

Next: Chapter 12 Practice
Your workbook for recognizing inherited relationship patterns

CHAPTER 12 PRACTICE

Breaking Inherited Patterns
Your workbook for recognizing what you inherited

Identify Your Inherited Patterns (The Full Picture)

Which patterns might have traveled through your family line? Check all that apply, remembering these could be genetic, learned, or both:

☐ Conflict avoidance (peace at any price)

☐ Explosive reactions (0 to 100)

☐ Emotional withdrawal (leaving when feelings arise)

☐ Hypervigilance (constant scanning)

☐ Conditional love ("I love you, but...")

☐ Perfectionism (never good enough)

☐ Enmeshment (no boundaries)

☐ Emotional absence (work over presence)

☐ Silent treatment (withdrawal as weapon)

☐ Guilt as control ("If you loved me...")

☐ Anxiety/worry patterns

☐ Depression/low mood tendencies

Potentially Inherited Strengths:

☐ Humor in hard times

☐ Persistence through challenges

☐ Creative problem-solving

☐ Ways of showing love

☐ Resilience strategies

☐ Cultural wisdom

☐ Survival skills

☐ Connection rituals

☐ Storytelling abilities

☐ Other: _____

Remember: You might share patterns with parents due to genetics, learning, similar environments, or coincidence. Don't assume direct transmission.

Map Your Generational Patterns (With Nuance)

From My Grandparents:

Patterns I've heard about or observed: _____

Strengths they developed to survive their circumstances: _____

What My Parents May Have Inherited:

Their challenges: _____

Their strengths: _____

How their patterns might have been adaptive for their lives: _____

What I Notice in Myself:

Patterns I share with family: _____

Patterns unique to me: _____

Strengths I've inherited or developed: _____

Consider multiple sources:

- Which patterns might be genetic? _____

- Which seem learned through observation? _____

- Which might be responses to similar stressors? _____

- Which came from peers/culture, not family? _____

Sibling Differences Check

If you have siblings, notice the differences:

I developed these patterns: _____

My sibling(s) developed: _____

We're different because: _____

This reminds you that inheritance isn't destiny—same family, different outcomes.

Practice Pattern Interruption

Choose ONE inherited pattern to work with this week:

The pattern I'll watch for: _____

How I'll recognize it starting:

Body sensations: _____

Familiar words rising: _____

Emotional signatures: _____

My interrupt phrase:

☐ "Wait, that's my mother's/father's voice"

☐ "I'm doing that thing"

☐ "This is the old pattern"

☐ "Let me choose differently"

☐ Other: _____

What I'll choose instead: _____

Remember: You won't catch it every time. Progress is noticing it sometimes, not perfection.

Daily Awareness Practice

Each day this week, notice ONE moment when an inherited pattern arises:

Day	Pattern I Noticed	Caught It?	What Happened?
Monday		Before/During/After/Didn't	
Tuesday		Before/During/After/Didn't	
Wednesday		Before/During/After/Didn't	
Thursday		Before/During/After/Didn't	
Friday		Before/During/After/Didn't	

Noticing after is still progress. Your brain is building new pathways each time you recognize a pattern.

The Both/And Practice

For each inherited pattern, practice holding both truths:

Pattern: _____ I inherited this tendency AND I have choice about it.

Pattern: _____ This came from my family AND I'm reshaping it.

Pattern: _____ I understand why my parents had this AND I can choose differently.

The Compassion Practice

Understanding doesn't excuse harm, but it can soften the edges:

My mother/primary caregiver gave me _____ because:

  □ That's what she knew

  □ She was doing her best with what she had

  □ She inherited it too

  □ She was surviving her own challenges

  □ That's what worked in her experience

My father/other caregiver gave me _____ because:

  □ That's what he knew

  □ He was doing his best with what he had

  □ He inherited it too

  □ He was surviving his own challenges

  □ That's what worked in his experience

I can have compassion for them while still:

☐ Choosing differently

☐ Protecting myself if needed

☐ Healing what hurts

☐ Breaking cycles

What You're Passing Forward (Or Not)

If you have or might have children:

Patterns I want to pass on: _____

Patterns I'm actively changing: _____

New patterns I'm creating: _____

If you don't have children:

Patterns I'm changing in all my relationships: _____

_____

How I'm influencing nieces/nephews/godchildren/friends: _____

_____

Remember: You're already changing patterns for future generations, whether or not you have children.

Agency Checkpoint

Fill in to remind yourself of your power:

☐ I inherited tendencies, not destinies

☐ My brain can form new patterns throughout life

☐ I actively interpret what I inherited

☐ I'm influenced by more than just my parents

☐ I have genetic traits AND behavioral choices

☐ Some patterns serve me and I can keep them

☐ Some patterns don't and I can change them

☐ Therapy can help if patterns feel stuck

☐ I'm already different from my parents in these ways: _____

_____

Tonight's Reflection

One inherited pattern I noticed today: _____

Whether it's genetic, learned, or both: _____

One inherited strength I used today: _____

One way I chose differently than my parents might have: _____

_____

I inherited patterns through genetics, learning, and environment. These are tendencies, not destinies. I also inherited strengths and resilience. I actively choose which patterns to keep or change. My siblings might have totally different patterns. Every moment of awareness creates possibility for change. I can have compassion for my parents while choosing differently. Professional help is available if patterns feel stuck. I'm already changing what gets passed forward.

Remember: You're not your mother's anxiety or your father's anger. You're not doomed to repeat their marriage. You might have inherited tendencies toward certain patterns, but you're constantly choosing—consciously or unconsciously—which ones to express, modify, or override.

Some patterns you'll interrupt easily. Others will take years to shift. Some might never fully go away but become manageable. And some inherited patterns—the humor, the persistence, the ways of showing love—you'll want to keep and strengthen.

The point isn't to erase your inheritance but to become conscious of it, so you can choose which parts serve you and which parts you're ready to transform.

* * *

Next: Chapter 13
Living with Nervous System Awareness

Living with Nervous System Awareness

Integration without overwhelm

THE MIDDLE PATH

Too much awareness: tracking every
breath, monitoring each heartbeat,
drowning in observation.

Too little awareness: patterns running wild,
body screaming unheard, unconscious
repetition.

The middle path: noticing when it matters,
forgetting when it doesn't,
living while aware.

Not hypervigilance turned inward.
Not oblivion either. Just enough attention
to catch what needs catching, release
what needs releasing, and sometimes—
blessed, necessary sometimes—
forget you're watching at all.

What Integration Actually Means

You've learned to notice your patterns. To read your body's signals. To catch inherited responses before they land. Now comes the real question: How do you live with this awareness without becoming obsessed with it?

The truth nobody tells you: awareness can become its own prison. You can get so good at tracking your nervous system that you forget to live. So vigilant about patterns that you create new ones. So focused on healing that healing becomes another way to stay broken.

I know because recently I caught myself monitoring Kyle's monitoring of himself. Meta-vigilance. We were both so busy noticing our patterns that we forgot to have an actual conversation.

"Mom," Kyle said, "I just noticed myself noticing my anxiety about noticing patterns." "I'm noticing you noticing that," I replied. We both burst out laughing. We'd disappeared into an awareness spiral, completely missing the present moment we were supposedly trying to be aware of.

The Research on Self-Monitoring

Studies on self-monitoring and mental health show a paradox: some awareness improves wellbeing, but excessive self-focus can increase anxiety and depression. Research on "self-focused attention" finds that:

Helpful awareness involves:

- Periodic check-ins with yourself
- Noticing patterns without judgment
- Using awareness to make conscious choices
- Maintaining focus on external life too

Harmful hypervigilance involves:

- Constant internal monitoring
- Judging every sensation and thought
- Awareness that increases anxiety
- Losing connection to external world

The sweet spot? Researchers suggest brief, intentional check-ins rather than constant monitoring. Think of it like checking your mirrors while driving—periodic glances, not staring at them constantly.

Signs You're Tipping Into Hypervigilance

You might be overdoing awareness if:

- You can't have a conversation without analyzing everyone's nervous system state
- You're exhausted from tracking patterns all day
- Your awareness practice creates more anxiety than it relieves
- You've stopped enjoying things because you're too busy noticing
- Every sensation becomes a problem to solve
- You judge yourself for not being aware enough
- You judge yourself for being too aware
- You can't remember the last time you just... existed

Last week I couldn't enjoy dinner because I was tracking my reaction to the food, Eric's mood, my breathing pattern, and whether I was in window or keyhole capacity. The meal passed without me tasting it.

Signs You're in the Sweet Spot

Healthy integration looks like:

- Noticing patterns when they matter, missing them when they don't

- Having awareness available but not always active

- Check-ins that inform choices without dominating attention

- Being able to forget about your nervous system for hours

- Enjoying experiences while occasionally noticing your state

- Using awareness to navigate challenges, not create them

- Sometimes being completely unconscious and that being fine

A Framework for Integration

Based on both research and practical experience, here's a structure for maintaining helpful awareness without drowning in it:

The 5-3-1 Rule

5 seconds in the morning: Quick body scan. How am I starting today? Window or keyhole? That's it.

3 times during the day: Brief check-ins during transitions (bathroom, lunch, driving). Just notice, don't analyze.

1 minute before bed: What patterns ran today? No judgment, just recognition.

Total daily awareness practice: Less than 5 minutes of focused attention.

Awareness-Free Zones

Designate certain activities as awareness-free:

My awareness-free zones:

- Watching movies (just watch)
- Playing with children (just play)
- During intimate moments (just connect)
- While creating art/music (just create)
- In nature (just be)

Kyle chose video games as his awareness-free zone. "When I'm gaming, I'm not tracking anything. My nervous system gets a break from being watched."

The Weekly Rhythm

Monday-Friday: Normal life with brief check-ins **Saturday:** One longer practice session (10-20 minutes) if desired **Sunday:** Complete awareness break—live unconsciously on purpose

This rhythm prevents both extremes: neglecting awareness and obsessing over it.

Real-World Integration Examples

Sarah (teacher): "I do a 10-second check between classes. Am I activated from the last group? Do I need to shake it off? Then I forget about it and teach."

Marcus (parent): "Morning check while making coffee. Quick reset in the car after drop-off. That's it. I can't parent while monitoring my nervous system."

Jennifer (nurse): "I notice if I'm catching patients' anxiety, but only during breaks. Can't do my job if I'm constantly tracking."

David (CEO): "Three breaths before big meetings to check my state. Otherwise, awareness would paralyze decision-making."

Notice: Everyone finds their own integration rhythm based on their life, not an ideal practice schedule.

When Awareness Disappears (And That's Okay)

You'll lose all awareness during:

- Crises (survival mode takes over)
- Intense joy (presence takes over)
- Deep focus (flow state takes over)
- Exhaustion (nothing left to notice with)
- Conflict (patterns run automatically)

This is normal. Integration isn't maintaining perfect awareness. It's noticing when you can, forgetting when you can't, and not judging either.

Two weeks ago, I had a massive argument with a family member. Every pattern ran. Doormat turned to dynamite. Three generations of conflict avoidance exploded into conflict escalation. Zero awareness during.

Two hours later, I thought: "Oh wow, that was quite the pattern parade." When I talked to Eric about it, he said: "At least you noticed afterward." "After counts," I told him.

The Community Element

Integration gets easier with others who understand this work:

Finding your people:

- Friends who get "window/keyhole days"
- Partners willing to notice patterns together
- Online communities discussing nervous system work
- Therapy or support groups
- Even one person who says "I do that too"

Kyle and Maddy now have pattern check-ins: "What ran today?" Not to fix, just to witness each other's awareness journey.

What community provides:

- Normalization (everyone has patterns)
- Accountability (gentle reminders to notice)
- Mirror (they see what you miss)
- Break from awareness (laughing about patterns together)
- Evidence of progress (they notice your changes)

Integration Troubleshooting

Problem: "I forget everything I've learned under stress" Solution: That's normal. Integration means remembering faster afterward, not perfect awareness during.

Problem: "My partner thinks this awareness stuff is weird" Solution: Use the language that works. "I'm stressed" instead of "I'm dysregulated." Results matter more than terminology.

Problem: "I'm aware but nothing changes" Solution: Awareness isn't magic. Sometimes you need additional support—therapy, medication, lifestyle changes. Awareness informs these choices.

Problem: "I judge myself for not being aware enough" Solution: The judging is just another pattern to notice. "Oh, there's my inner critic about awareness. Hello, old friend."

The Long-Term Journey

Integration happens in spirals, not straight lines:

Year 1: Excited about awareness, practice constantly, overwhelm yourself, back off

Year 2: Find rhythm, forget for months, remember again, gentler practice

Year 3: Natural rhythm emerges, awareness becomes background hum

Year 4+: Use awareness when needed, forget when not, no longer "practicing"—just living with more choice

I'm in year 5. Still checking locks sometimes. But now it's: check, notice I'm checking, laugh, check once more, move on. The pattern runs but doesn't rule.

What Success Actually Looks Like

Integrated awareness isn't:

- Constant monitoring
- Never having patterns

- Perfect regulation

- Always conscious

Integrated awareness is:

- Noticing enough to have choice sometimes
- Patterns running with less intensity
- Recovering faster when activated
- Remembering you have tools (even if you forget to use them)
- Being kind to yourself about the whole messy process

Kyle last week: "I had a panic attack. Full blown. But I noticed it starting, told Maddy, used my tools after. Still panicked, but differently."

That's integration—not prevention of all patterns, but conscious participation when possible.

Your Integration Practice

Start simple:

This week, try:

- Morning: 5-second check-in
- Day: Notice during one transition
- Evening: "What ran today?" (no judgment)
- Weekend: One awareness-free activity

Next month, maybe:

- Add a midday check-in
- Find one person to share patterns with
- Notice one pattern with compassion

Eventually:

- Natural rhythm emerges
- Awareness becomes available but not constant
- You remember when it matters, forget when it doesn't

Remember This

- The middle path between hypervigilance and oblivion is narrow and personal
- Research shows brief check-ins work better than constant monitoring
- 5-3-1 rule: 5 seconds morning, 3 transitions, 1 minute evening
- Awareness-free zones are essential for integration
- Losing awareness during stress is normal, not failure
- Community makes integration easier
- Success is having choice sometimes, not awareness always
- Integration happens in spirals over years
- Be gentle with yourself about the whole process

The goal was never to become a nervous system monitoring machine. It was to have enough awareness to make conscious choices when it matters, and to forget about it entirely when it doesn't.

Some days you'll track everything. Some days you'll track nothing. Most days you'll land somewhere in between—aware enough to navigate challenges, unconscious enough to enjoy your life.

That's the middle path. That's integration. That's enough.

* * *

Next: Chapter 13 Practice
Living with Nervous System Awareness

CHAPTER 13 PRACTICE

Living with Nervous System Awareness
Your workbook for finding balance

The Awareness Check-In

Right now, before reading further, notice: Are you tracking your breath? Monitoring your shoulders? Analyzing your state?

If yes, that's fine. But also notice: Has awareness become another thing to be perfect at?

This chapter is about finding the sweet spot between knowing and not needing to know all the time.

Signs of Too Much vs. Just Right

Check which describes you lately:

Too Much Awareness (Hypervigilance):

☐ I analyze every sensation

☐ I can't enjoy things because I'm monitoring

□ I'm exhausted from tracking myself

□ I judge myself for having patterns

□ Awareness makes me more anxious

□ I've lost spontaneity

□ I track everyone else's nervous system too

□ I can't remember when I last just... existed

Just Right (Integration):

□ I notice patterns when they matter

□ I can forget about awareness for hours

□ Brief check-ins are enough

□ I'm kind about patterns I notice

□ Awareness helps me navigate challenges

□ I still have spontaneous moments

□ Others' states don't consume me

□ I regularly just exist without monitoring

Too Little (Unconscious):

□ Patterns run me completely

☐ I only notice after big crashes

☐ My body's signals surprise me

☐ Same problems keep repeating

☐ I feel out of control often

☐ No idea what triggers me

☐ Can't recognize patterns at all

Most of us swing between all three. That's normal.

Your Personal 5-3-1 Practice

Let's make this realistic for YOUR life:

My 5-second morning check will be:

☐ While coffee brews

☐ Before getting out of bed

☐ In the shower

☐ During commute

☐ Other: _____

My 3 transition check-ins will be:

1.

2.

3.

(Examples: bathroom breaks, before meals, walking to car, between meetings)

My 1-minute evening reflection will be:

☐ While brushing teeth

☐ In bed before sleep

☐ After dinner

☐ While walking dog

☐ Other: _____

Remember: Total time = less than 5 minutes daily. That's it.

Declare Your Awareness-Free Zones

Choose 3-5 activities where you'll deliberately NOT monitor anything:

☐ Watching TV/movies

☐ Playing with kids/pets

□ Exercise

□ Sex/intimacy

□ Creative activities

□ Gaming

□ Reading

□ Cooking

□ Nature time

□ Conversations with: _____

□ Other: _____

□ Other: _____

Permission granted to be completely unconscious during these.

Integration Troubleshooting

Which of these is your biggest challenge?

□ I forget everything under stress → That's normal. Success is remembering faster afterward, not perfect awareness during.

□ I can't stop monitoring everything → Set a timer. Five minutes of awareness, then mandatory break. Build unconscious time.

□ My partner/friends think this is weird → Use normal language. "I'm stressed" not "I'm dysregulated." Results matter more than terminology.

□ Nothing seems to change despite awareness → Awareness isn't magic. It informs other changes—therapy, medication, lifestyle. What else might help?

□ I judge myself constantly → The judgment is just another pattern. "Oh, hello inner critic about my awareness. You're a pattern too."

Your Integration Experiment This Week

Pick just ONE to try:

□ The 5-3-1 practice (5 sec morning, 3 quick checks, 1 min evening)

□ One awareness-free activity daily

□ Share one pattern with someone ("I noticed I do this thing...")

□ Notice without fixing (just observe, no pressure to change)

□ Catch yourself monitoring and gently stop

□ Forget about all of this for a day and see what happens

Finding Your People

Who in your life might understand this work?

People who might get "window/keyhole days": _____

Someone I could share patterns with: _____

Online communities to explore: _____

Professional support to consider: _____

Even one person who gets it changes everything.

The Reality Check Questions

Answer honestly:

Has awareness work become another way to feel broken?

Yes / No / Sometimes

Do I spend more time monitoring than living?

Yes / No / Sometimes

Am I kinder to myself since starting this work?

Yes / No / Sometimes

Can I forget about patterns and just enjoy things?

Yes / No / Sometimes

If you answered "No" to the last two, time to ease up. Awareness should increase compassion and presence, not decrease them.

Your Long-Term Vision

In one year, I hope my awareness practice looks like:

_____

Signs I'll know I've found balance:

_____

What I want to remember when I forget everything:

_____

This Week's Simple Practice

Each day, just notice:

Monday: Did I have any awareness today? Y/N (Both are fine)

Tuesday: Did I have any awareness today? Y/N

Wednesday: Did I have any awareness today? Y/N

Thursday: Did I have any awareness today? Y/N

Friday: Did I have any awareness today? Y/N

Weekend: Did I forget about awareness? Y/N (Yes is good!)

No judgment. Just noticing if you noticed.

Permission Slips

Sign off on these permissions for yourself:

    ☐ Permission to forget everything I've learned

    ☐ Permission to have patterns forever

□ Permission to stop monitoring

□ Permission to be unconscious sometimes

□ Permission to be imperfect at awareness

□ Permission to find this work weird

□ Permission to take breaks

□ Permission to be human

Signed: _____

Date: _____

Tonight's One Question

Am I using awareness to be kind to myself or to have another thing to perfect?

_____

If it's become another perfection project, time to ease up. Way up.

TAKE AWAY

Integration means just enough awareness to have choice sometimes. Not constant monitoring. Not perfect patterns. Not always conscious

The 5-3-1 rule: 5 seconds morning, 3 quick checks, 1 minute evening. That's it. Less than 5 minutes total.

Awareness-free zones are essential. Losing awareness under stress is normal. Finding even one person who gets it helps.

Some days you'll track everything. Some days nothing. Both are fine.

The goal was never perfection. It was occasional choice. And kindness toward yourself.

That's enough. That's integration. That's the whole practice.

Listen, I wrote this integration practice while simultaneously monitoring my breathing, checking my capacity, and noticing my shoulders rising. The irony isn't lost on me.

But here's what I'm learning: we don't need to be awareness ninjas. We need to be slightly more conscious humans who occasionally catch patterns and sometimes make different choices. That's it. That's the whole thing.

Tomorrow I might forget everything in this workbook. Next week I might remember one thing. Both outcomes are completely fine. The awareness that matters isn't constant—it's just available when you really need it.

And honestly? Sometimes the most aware thing you can do is forget about awareness entirely and just live your life. That's not failure. That's integration.

EPILOGUE

The Ongoing Journey

What you've discovered and what comes next

You picked up this book because something in your body wouldn't settle.

Maybe you were checking locks five times before bed. Maybe you were floating near the ceiling during conversations. Maybe you kept saying yes when your shoulders screamed no.

You've traveled through thirteen chapters. You've met Kyle checking his locks, learning to notice his patterns. You've seen Maddy learning not to catch his panic. You've watched us all stumble through this messy process of awareness.

Now what?

The Science of What You've Built

Here's what the research tells us about what you've actually accomplished: The simple act of noticing—what neuroscientists call

275

metacognitive awareness—accounts for 45-55% of all therapeutic change, regardless of the specific treatment approach. This isn't a small effect. It's the primary mechanism driving healing across virtually all effective mental health interventions.

Remember Chapter 1, when you learned to notice the difference between having anxiety and being consumed by it? That tiny gap—"oh, I'm doing that checking thing again"—wasn't just the beginning. It was already changing your brain.

Sara Lazar's Harvard research shows that just eight weeks of awareness practice produces measurable increases in gray matter density in the hippocampus, your brain's emotional regulation center. Yi-Yuan Tang's studies push this further, documenting white matter changes in attention networks within just 2-4 weeks of practice. These aren't subtle statistical findings—they represent fundamental rewiring of how your brain processes emotion and attention.

Every time you've noticed:

- Your shoulders rising before saying yes (Chapter 9)
- Your body syncing with someone's anxiety (Chapter 10)
- That volcanic rage about the spoon being 90% old wound (Chapter 11)
- Your mother's words coming from your mouth (Chapter 12)

You've been literally reshaping your neural architecture. The anterior cingulate cortex strengthening its connections. The amygdala—your fear center—actually shrinking. The prefrontal regions that enable choice growing denser.

Why Awareness Helps You Heal

One of the most powerful skills for recovery is simple: noticing your thoughts and feelings without getting pulled into them. Instead of treating every thought like absolute truth, you learn to see it as something that comes and goes—like watching clouds pass without chasing them.

Back in 2007, researchers discovered that people who practiced this kind of noticing were *less likely to slip back into depression* after treatment. Therapy that encouraged awareness of thoughts built this skill sometimes even more effectively than medication alone. A few years later, in 2012, another study showed that mindfulness training helped people get better at observing their thoughts—and those who improved the most at this stayed healthier over time.

Since then, studies across both depression and anxiety show the same pattern: **awareness of your inner experience—just noticing without judgment—protects your mental health**. Most recently, in 2022, scientists confirmed that people who developed this awareness were *less likely to relapse a year later*.

In short, learning to notice what's happening inside you—without rushing to believe it or fix it—makes recovery both stronger and more lasting.

What Progress Really Looks Like

Kyle called yesterday. "Mom, I had a terrible week. Checked locks twenty times. Had three panic attacks. Snapped at Maddy."

"And?"

"And I noticed all of it. While it was happening. That's different, right?"

That's exactly different. Research on decentering—the ability to observe thoughts and feelings as temporary mental events rather than absolute truths—shows this capacity is the strongest predictor of recovery. In a major trial with 227 participants, increases in decentering (exactly what Kyle is describing) predicted remission from depression more powerfully than any other factor.

Real Progress Is:

- Catching patterns three seconds sooner

- Recovering in two hours instead of two days

- Saying "sorry, that was my old pattern" instead of defending it

- Having one moment of choice where there used to be none

- Recognizing "I'm in freeze" even while frozen

- Building what researchers call "response flexibility"—that space Viktor Frankl wrote about between stimulus and response

Real Progress Is NOT:

- Never getting triggered

- Always staying calm

- Perfect boundaries every time

- Elimination of all patterns

- Constant awareness

- Feeling "healed"

The Transdiagnostic Power of Awareness

What you've been building through this book—awareness—isn't just helpful for one specific issue. It's what researchers call a "transdiagnostic mechanism," meaning it works across different conditions and challenges.

The Unified Protocol studies show that developing emotional awareness helps equally whether someone struggles with:

- Anxiety (like checking locks repeatedly)

- Depression (that stone state from Chapter 8)

- Trauma responses (leaving your body, Chapter 4)

- Relationship patterns (the doormat/dynamite responses, Chapter 9)

Adrian Wells' research on metacognitive therapy found effect sizes of g = 1.72 — enormous by psychological intervention standards. What was the key ingredient? Teaching people to notice their patterns of worry and rumination without being consumed by them. Exactly what you've been practicing.

The Body-Brain Integration

Remember Chapter 3, when you learned your gut contains 500 million neurons? Or Chapter 7, when you discovered your night guard won't let you sleep because your body doesn't believe it's safe?

This isn't metaphor. Sarah Garfinkel and Hugo Critchley's research on interoception—your ability to sense internal bodily signals—shows that individuals with better body awareness have increased gray matter volume in the right anterior insula, along with better emotional regulation capacity.

When you found your neutral spot in Chapter 4 (that boring elbow or calm earlobe), you were rebuilding interoceptive awareness from the ground up. Studies show this single practice—finding one safe zone in the body—can begin recalibrating an entire nervous system disrupted by trauma.

The Relational Rewiring

Part Three took you into the advanced territory—awareness in relationship. The mirror neuron research, while still being mapped in humans, suggests why this is so challenging and so important. When you noticed yourself syncing with others' anxiety (Chapter 10) or recognized inherited patterns rising (Chapter 12), you were working with deeply embedded neural networks designed for survival through social connection.

But here's what's remarkable: that moment Kyle caught himself about to say "you're being too sensitive"—his grandmother's words about to emerge through two generations—and chose differently? He was literally interrupting an intergenerational neural pathway and creating a new one.

Peter Fonagy's research on mentalization shows that developing awareness of mental states (yours and others') can actually change attachment patterns previously thought to be fixed. That 70% correspondence between parent and child attachment styles? The 30% who develop different patterns do so through exactly the kind of awareness you've been building.

Tomorrow's Pattern, Tomorrow's Choice

Tomorrow, someone will ask you for something. Your mouth might say yes before you check with your body. But now—here's what's different—you'll notice three seconds later: "I did it again."

Those three seconds matter more than you might realize. Research on neuroplasticity shows that the moment of recognition—even after the pattern has run—is when new neural pathways begin forming. The noticing itself, even delayed, is rewiring your brain.

Or your partner will walk in stressed and you'll match their energy completely. An hour later you'll think: "Wait, I was fine before they arrived." That recognition is your prefrontal cortex coming back online, creating what researchers call "cognitive reappraisal capacity."

The Minimum Effective Dose

One of the most practically significant findings challenges our assumptions about how much awareness practice is needed. Studies show that even 3-5 minute practices can produce measurable improvements. A study comparing 10-minute versus 20-minute sessions found no significant difference in outcomes.

This is why the 5-3-1 practice from Chapter 13 works:

- 5 seconds in the morning

- 3 brief check-ins during transitions

- 1 minute before bed

Less than 5 minutes total, but enough to maintain the neural pathways you've been building.

What Stays True

The neuroscience confirms what you've experienced: awareness isn't just one technique among many. It's the fundamental capacity underlying emotional health.

Studies examining therapeutic change across all modalities—cognitive-behavioral, psychodynamic, somatic, mindfulness-based—find the same thing: the development of observing capacity predicts outcomes better than any specific technique.

You're not alone in this. The research suggests these patterns are nearly universal:

- 70% of people experience imposter syndrome

- Attachment patterns affect most relationships

- Emotional contagion happens to everyone (though sensitivity varies)

- Inherited patterns show up across cultures

We're all checking locks, leaving our bodies, saying yes when we mean no. We're all learning to notice. The science shows this isn't pathology—it's human nervous system responding to a complex world.

The Ongoing Evolution

Neuroplasticity research reveals something both challenging and hopeful: your brain remains capable of change throughout your entire life, but this capacity works both ways. Old patterns can strengthen without practice; new patterns need reinforcement.

This is why the work continues. Not because you're broken and need endless fixing, but because awareness is like physical fitness—it's maintained through practice, not achieved once and kept forever.

Those small moments—catching yourself mid-pattern, choosing differently even once, repairing after rupture—accumulate into measurable brain changes. The strengthened prefrontal-amygdala pathways that provide emotional regulation. The enhanced insula development supporting emotional granularity. The reduced default mode network activity associated with less rumination.

One Last Thing

The research is remarkably consistent: the observer capacity you've been developing—the ability to notice without being consumed—is more powerful than any specific therapeutic technique.

But here's what the studies can't capture: the moment you realize you're not broken. The first time you catch a pattern and choose differently. The day you recognize your mother's anxiety rising in your chest and consciously decide not to pass it to your children.

These moments aren't just personal victories. They're evolutionary. Each conscious choice ripples forward, changing not just your neural pathways but potentially affecting epigenetic expression, attachment patterns in future relationships, and the emotional inheritance of the next generation.

You have anxiety sometimes, but you're also the part that notices the anxiety. You have patterns, but you're also the part that sees them. That noticing part? It's been here the whole time. The science tells us it's changing your brain. Your experience tells you it's changing your life. Both are true.

From one person checking locks to another.
From someone who floats near ceilings to someone who might.
From a mother who inherited vigilance to anyone breaking
inherited patterns.

You have everything you need.
It's in your capacity to notice.
It's in that split second of recognition.
It's in your willingness to keep trying, imperfectly, tomorrow.

The work continues as long as we're breathing.
Pattern by pattern. Breath by breath. Moment by moment.

Keep noticing.

— With love, ongoing practice, and deep respect
for your rewiring brain,

Joy

* * *

RESOURCES

Recommended Reading

A Note About These Resources

The books and resources listed here explore themes similar to those in this book. They represent various approaches to understanding trauma, the nervous system, and healing. Some present well-established research, others describe clinical frameworks that practitioners find useful, and still others offer theoretical models that remain debated in the scientific community.

No single approach works for everyone. What matters is whether a framework helps you understand your experience and supports positive change. Take what serves you, leave what doesn't, and always trust your own experience above any expert's theory.

RESOURCES & RESEARCH REFERENCES

Research Citations

Neuroscience of Awareness and Brain Changes

Gray Matter and Structural Changes:

- Lazar, S. W., Kerr, C. E., Wasserman, R. H., et al. (2005). Meditation experience is associated with increased cortical thickness. *NeuroReport*, 16(17), 1893-1897. [Referenced in Epilogue]

- Hölzel, B. K., Carmody, J., Vangel, M., et al. (2011). Mindfulness practice leads to increases in regional brain gray matter density. *Psychiatry Research: Neuroimaging*, 191(1), 36-43. [Referenced in Epilogue]

White Matter Changes:

- Tang, Y. Y., Lu, Q., Geng, X., et al. (2010). Short-term meditation induces white matter changes in the anterior cingulate. *Proceedings of the National Academy of Sciences*, 107(35), 15649-15652. [Referenced in Epilogue]

Metacognitive Awareness and Therapeutic Change

Decentering and Depression:

- Fresco, D. M., Moore, M. T., van Dulmen, M. H., et al. (2007). Initial psychometric properties of the Experiences Questionnaire: Validation of a self-report measure of decentering. *Behavior Therapy*, 38(3), 234-246. [Referenced in Epilogue - 2007 studies]

- Teasdale, J. D., Moore, R. G., Hayhurst, H., et al. (2002). Metacognitive awareness and prevention of relapse in depression: Empirical evidence. *Journal of Consulting and Clinical Psychology*, 70(2), 275-287. [Foundation for Chapter 1 concepts]

Mindfulness-Based Interventions:

- Goldberg, S. B., Riordan, K. M., Sun, S., & Davidson, R. J. (2022). The empirical status of mindfulness-based interventions: A systematic review of 44 meta-analyses of randomized controlled trials. *Perspectives on Psychological Science*, 17(1), 108-130. [Referenced in Epilogue - 2022 studies]

- Segal, Z. V., Williams, J. M. G., & Teasdale, J. D. (2012). *Mindfulness-Based Cognitive Therapy for Depression* (2nd ed.). Guilford Press. [Referenced in Epilogue - 2012 studies]

Trauma and Nervous System Regulation

Polyvagal Theory:

- Porges, S. W. (2011). *The Polyvagal Theory: Neurophysiological Foundations of Emotions, Attachment, Communication, and Self-Regulation*. Norton. [Referenced in Chapters 7, 10]

- Dana, D. (2018). *The Polyvagal Theory in Therapy: Engaging the Rhythm of Regulation*. Norton. [Clinical applications referenced throughout]

Trauma and the Body:

- van der Kolk, B. A. (2014). *The Body Keeps the Score: Brain, Mind, and Body in the Healing of Trauma*. Viking. [Foundation for Part One concepts]

- Levine, P. A. (1997). *Waking the Tiger: Healing Trauma*. North Atlantic Books. [Referenced in Chapter 8 - discharge concepts]

Attachment and Relationships

Attachment Patterns:

- Main, M., & Solomon, J. (1986). Discovery of an insecure-disorganized/disoriented attachment pattern. In T. B. Brazelton & M. W. Yogman (Eds.), *Affective Development in Infancy* (pp. 95-124). Ablex. [70% correspondence statistic - Chapter 12]

- Siegel, D. J. (2012). *The Developing Mind: How Relationships and the Brain Interact to Shape Who We Are* (2nd ed.). Guilford Press. [Referenced in Chapter 12]

Earned Secure Attachment:

- Roisman, G. I., Padrón, E., Sroufe, L. A., & Egeland, B. (2002). Earned-secure attachment status in retrospect and prospect. *Child Development*, 73(4), 1204-1219. [Referenced in Chapter 12]

Specific Research Topics

Emotional Contagion:

- Hatfield, E., Cacioppo, J. T., & Rapson, R. L. (1994). *Emotional Contagion*. Cambridge University Press. [Chapter 10 foundation]

- Prochazkova, E., & Kret, M. E. (2017). Connecting minds and sharing emotions through mimicry: A neurocognitive model of emotional contagion. *Neuroscience & Biobehavioral Reviews*, 80, 99-114. [Chapter 10]

Mirror Neurons:

- Rizzolatti, G., & Craighero, L. (2004). The mirror-neuron

system. *Annual Review of Neuroscience*, 27, 169-192. [Referenced in Chapters 10, 12]

- Note: Human mirror neuron research remains contested. See Hickok, G. (2014). *The Myth of Mirror Neurons*. Norton, for critical perspective.

Interoception:

- Craig, A. D. (2009). How do you feel—now? The anterior insula and human awareness. *Nature Reviews Neuroscience*, 10(1), 59-70. [Chapter 4 - body awareness]

- Garfinkel, S. N., & Critchley, H. D. (2013). Interoception, emotion and brain: New insights link internal physiology to social behaviour. *Social Cognitive and Affective Neuroscience*, 8(3), 231-234. [Referenced in Epilogue]

Highly Sensitive Persons (HSPs):

- Aron, E. N., & Aron, A. (1997). Sensory-processing sensitivity and its relation to introversion and emotionality. *Journal of Personality and Social Psychology*, 73(2), 345-368. [Chapter 10]

- Aron, E. N. (2016). *The Highly Sensitive Person*. Broadway Books. [Referenced in Chapters 6, 10]

Imposter Syndrome:

- Clance, P. R., & Imes, S. A. (1978). The imposter phenomenon in high achieving women: Dynamics and therapeutic intervention. *Psychotherapy: Theory, Research & Practice*, 15(3), 241-247. [Original research]

- Bravata, D. M., Watts, S. A., Keefer, A. L., et al. (2020). Prevalence, predictors, and treatment of impostor syndrome: A systematic review. *Journal of General Internal Medicine*, 35(4), 1252-1275. [70% prevalence - Chapters 2, 12]

Sleep and Hypervigilance

PTSD and Sleep:

- Germain, A. (2013). Sleep disturbances as the hallmark of PTSD: Where are we now? *American Journal of Psychiatry*, 170(4), 372-382. [Chapter 7]

- Krakow, B., & Zadra, A. (2006). Clinical management of chronic nightmares: Imagery rehearsal therapy. *Behavioral Sleep Medicine*, 4(1), 45-70. [Chapter 7 - night guard concept]

Exercise and Mental Health

Exercise Benefits and Limitations:

- Schuch, F. B., Vancampfort, D., Richards, J., et al. (2016). Exercise as a treatment for depression: A meta-analysis adjusting for publication bias. *Journal of Psychiatric Research*, 77, 42-51. [Chapter 8]

- Stanton, R., & Reaburn, P. (2014). Exercise and the treatment of depression: A review of the exercise program variables. *Journal of Science and Medicine in Sport*, 17(2), 177-182. [Chapter 8 - context effects]

Minimum Effective Dose:

- Fogg, B. J. (2019). *Tiny Habits: The Small Changes That Change Everything*. Houghton Mifflin Harcourt. [Part Two - tiny adjustments concept]

Recommended Books with Chapter Relevance

Foundational Texts

The Body Keeps the Score by Bessel van der Kolk, MD (2014)

- Comprehensive overview of trauma's effects on body and brain
- Relevant to: All chapters, especially Part One (recognizing patterns) and Chapter 3 (body symptoms)
- Note: While neuroscience sections are well-documented, some therapeutic approaches have varying levels of evidence

Waking the Tiger by Peter Levine (1997)

- Introduces Somatic Experiencing and incomplete survival responses
- Relevant to: Chapter 8 (discharge through movement), Chapter 4 (finding safety in the body)
- Note: Animal model comparisons are theoretical frameworks, not proven mechanisms

Nervous System Regulation

Polyvagal Theory in Therapy by Deb Dana (2018)

- Clinical applications of polyvagal theory
- Relevant to: Chapter 7 (night guard and safety), Chapter 10 (co-regulation)
- Note: Polyvagal theory is widely used but continues to face scientific scrutiny

The Body Remembers by Babette Rothschild (2000)

- Integration of neuroscience and body psychotherapy
- Relevant to: Chapter 3 (body symptoms), Chapter 4 (finding neutral zones)

Attachment and Relationships

Attached by Amir Levine and Rachel Heller (2010)

- Accessible introduction to adult attachment
- Relevant to: Part Three (all relationship chapters)
- Note: Attachment styles are more fluid than categories suggest

Hold Me Tight by Sue Johnson (2008)

- Emotionally Focused Therapy for couples
- Relevant to: Chapter 10 (emotional syncing), Chapter 11 (relationship dynamics)

Mindfulness and Awareness

Full Catastrophe Living by Jon Kabat-Zinn (1990)

- Foundation text on Mindfulness-Based Stress Reduction (MBSR)
- Relevant to: All chapters on awareness and noticing
- Note: Individual responses to mindfulness vary significantly

The Mindful Way Through Depression by Williams, Teasdale, Segal, and Kabat-Zinn (2007)

- Mindfulness-Based Cognitive Therapy (MBCT)
- Relevant to: Chapter 1 (observer capacity), Chapter 13 (integration)
- Strong research support for preventing depression relapse

Additional Support Resources

Crisis Resources

- 988 Suicide & Crisis Lifeline (call or text 988)
- Crisis Text Line (text HOME to 741741)
- International crisis lines: findahelpline.com

Professional Organizations

- International Society for Traumatic Stress Studies (istss.org)
- National Center for PTSD (ptsd.va.gov)
- Anxiety and Depression Association of America (adaa.org)

Finding Trauma-Informed Therapists

- Psychology Today Therapist Directory (filter for trauma-informed)
- EMDR International Association (emdria.org) - for EMDR therapists
- Somatic Experiencing International (traumahealing.org)

Online Communities (Use with Caution)

- r/CPTSD (Reddit) - Complex PTSD support
- The Mighty - Mental health community
- Note: Online spaces vary in quality and can sometimes increase symptoms

Apps and Tools

- Insight Timer - Free meditation with awareness practices

- How We Feel - Emotional awareness tracking

- Sanvello - Mood tracking and coping tools

- Note: Apps supplement but don't replace professional support

Important Considerations

About Research:

- Scientific understanding evolves rapidly in neuroscience and trauma fields

- Effect sizes and specific percentages should be viewed as estimates

- Individual responses vary significantly from research averages

- Cultural context affects all interventions

About Books and Resources:

- Books by researchers tend toward caution; popular books may overstate claims

- Personal accounts provide valuable insights even without proven mechanisms

- Western-developed approaches may not translate universally

- What helps one person may not help another

About This Book's Approach:

- Combines peer-reviewed research with clinical observations and lived experience

- Some frameworks (window/keyhole days, night guard) are practical tools, not scientific categories

- Personal examples are composites for privacy while illustrating patterns

- Practices are meant to complement, never replace, professional care

Chapter-Specific Research Notes

- **Chapter 1:** Observer capacity draws from metacognitive awareness research

- **Chapter 2:** Inner protector concept informed by Internal Family Systems and parts work

- **Chapter 3:** Somatic symptoms supported by psychosomatic medicine research

- **Chapter 4:** Neutral zones inspired by Somatic Experiencing and body-based therapies

- **Chapter 5:** Window of tolerance from trauma therapy (Siegel, 1999)

- **Chapter 6:** Anxiety types based on clinical observation, not diagnostic categories

- **Chapter 7:** Night guard metaphor created for this book, based on hypervigilance research

- **Chapter 8:** Movement patterns are observational categories, not scientific classifications

- **Chapter 9:** Doormat/dynamite framework is author's model based on clinical patterns

- **Chapter 10:** Emotional contagion research is established; individual susceptibility varies

- **Chapter 11:** The 10/90 framework is author's tool, not researched formula

- **Chapter 12:** Intergenerational transmission includes genetic, behavioral, and environmental factors

- **Chapter 13:** Integration timeline based on author's observation, not research

* * *

Note: This resource list represents knowledge through 2024. The science of trauma, nervous system regulation, and mental health continues to evolve. Always consult current research and qualified professionals for the most up-to-date information.

QUICK REFERENCE

Complete Key Practices

These are all the core practices from the book, simplified for quick reference. Return to the full chapters for detailed instructions and context.

Remember the foundation: *Notice first, validate second, only then try to adjust.*

Part One: Recognition Practices

The Pattern Recognition Practice (Chapter 1)

- Catch yourself in a pattern
- Say: "Oh, there's [pattern]. Hello, old friend."
- Notice who's noticing
- Wonder when it first helped
- Continue your day

Notice Response to Good Things (Chapter 2)

- Morning: Set intention to notice
- During day: Pause when good things happen
- Evening: Note without judgment

The Body Check-In (Chapter 3)

- Three times daily: Notice jaw, shoulders, stomach
- Don't change, just notice
- Awareness before release

The Neutral Spot Wonder (Chapter 4)

- Find one boring/neutral body part
- Rest attention there briefly
- Remember: observer is always neutral

Part Two: Working Practices

Capacity Check (Chapter 5)

- Morning: Window or keyhole day?
- Adjust schedule accordingly
- Honor actual capacity

Anxiety Acknowledgment (Chapter 6)

- "I'm anxious about [specific thing]"
- "This makes sense because [reason]"
- "My body is protecting me from [risk]"
- Then try physical regulation

Thank Your Night Guard (Chapter 7)

- Recognize guard on duty
- Thank for protection
- Update about current safety

- Give permission to rest

Movement Medicine (Chapter 8)

- Activated state → Discharge movement
- Exhausted state → Tiny movements or rest
- Disconnected state → Grounding movement
- Balanced state → Whatever feels good

Part Three: Relationship Practices

Boundary Awareness (Chapter 9)

- Notice which tool: Doormat/Dynamite/Disappear
- Find the space between trigger and response
- Ask: "What is anger protecting?"

Syncing Check (Chapter 10)

- Before: Notice baseline
- During: Notice syncing
- Choose: Match or maintain?
- After: Reset if needed

Intensity Math (Chapter 11)

- Notice overreaction
- Ask: "How old does this feel?"
- Consider all factors: current, past, physical state

Pattern Interrupt (Chapter 12)

- Notice inherited words rising
- Catch mid-sentence
- Say: "That's not my voice"
- Choose differently

Integration Balance (Chapter 13)

- Morning: 5-second check
- Transitions: Brief notice
- Evening: 1-minute reflection
- Rest: Forget and live

GLOSSARY

Terms and concepts used throughout this book, defined in the context of nervous system awareness and patterns. These definitions reflect how we use these terms in our exploration of awareness, not necessarily their clinical or academic meanings.

Allostatic Overload
When your stress response system exhausts itself from being activated too long. Like a smoke alarm that's been shrieking until the battery dies.

Body Mapping
The unique way your individual body stores and expresses emotional experiences through physical sensations. Your personal symptom dictionary.

Capacity/Window of Tolerance
The range where you can handle stress without becoming overwhelmed or shutting down. Changes daily based on sleep, stress, and other factors.

Co-regulation
How nervous systems regulate through connection with others. Can be positive (calm person steadies anxious one) or negative (catching someone's stress).

Doormat Response
Automatically saying yes to avoid conflict, disappointing others, or

triggering abandonment. One of three main boundary tools.

Dual Awareness
Knowing you're here now while recognizing a feeling is from then. "I'm safe AND my body remembers when I wasn't."

Dynamite Response
Explosive boundaries that create maximum distance through anger or cutting people off. Another main boundary tool.

Earned Secure Attachment
Developing secure attachment patterns through healing work, even without receiving secure attachment in childhood.

Emotional Contagion
The tendency to synchronize with others' emotional states through various mechanisms including mimicry and unconscious calibration.

Enteric Nervous System
The network of about 500 million neurons in your gut, often called the "second brain."

Hypervigilance
Being on high alert all the time, constantly scanning for danger even when safe. Your internal security guard who won't take a break.

Implicit Memory
Body memories stored as sensations and automatic responses rather than conscious recollections. Why you react like your parent without choosing to.

Imposter Syndrome
The feeling that you're a fraud who will be "found out," even when you've earned your success. About 70% of people experience this.

Keyhole Day
A day when your window of tolerance is tiny. Everything feels too much. Even small tasks feel impossible.

Lightning State
When anxiety/agitation creates buzzing energy that needs discharge through vigorous movement.

Mirror Neurons
Brain cells that fire both when you do something and when you watch someone else do it. Their exact role in humans is still being studied.

Neuroplasticity
The brain's ability to form new neural pathways throughout life. Why change is possible at any age.

Observer Capacity
The part of you that can notice what you're thinking or feeling without being completely consumed by it.

Polyvagal Theory
A clinical framework for understanding how the nervous system shifts between states of safety, danger, and life-threat. Explains freeze, fight, flight responses.

Proactive Boundaries
Boundaries set in advance based on values/needs, communicated from a centered place. Bypass doormat/dynamite patterns.

Protective Patterns
Behaviors your body learned to keep you safe, which might keep running even when you don't need them anymore.

Reactive Boundaries
Split-second responses when someone makes a request, often driven by body patterns from past experiences.

Somatic
Related to the body. Somatic symptoms are physical symptoms arising from emotional causes.

Stone State
Depression/shutdown state where body feels impossibly heavy. Needs tiny movements to gradually reactivate.

The Space Between
The pause between stimulus and response where choice becomes possible—when you can notice it.

Window Day
A day when your window of tolerance is wide. You can handle complexity, help others, make decisions clearly.

GRATITUDE

ACKNOWLEDGMENTS

This book exists because of the courage and trust of several people who allowed their struggles to become part of something potentially useful to others.

Kyle — For your willingness to let me share our ongoing journey, knowing that healing isn't linear and progress includes setbacks. Your courage in allowing these imperfect, in-process stories to be told makes this book honest. We're both still working on our patterns. That's the whole point.

Maddy — For your patience with our family's learning curve and for being Kyle's anchor when his nervous system needed steady ground. Your perspective kept us honest about what actually helps versus what we wished would help.

Eric — My patient husband, who gave me the space to learn an entirely new field and translate complex medical and psychological concepts into something accessible. Your support allowed this project to exist.

Tim — My sounding board and editor when I kept changing my perspective after reading something different in additional research. Your patience through countless revisions helped shape this into something coherent.

Dr. Jessica Wei — For teaching me through your own healing journey. Your parallel path with Kyle's—both brilliant, constantly self-improving, and courageously honest about the messy reality of recovery—illuminated patterns I might have missed. Your willingness to share your struggles confirmed that Kyle was not unique and healing was not linear.

Jay Johansen — Whose paintings grace this book. Your art does what my words try to do—bypass the thinking mind to speak directly to the wounded places.

* * *

To the thousands of patients whose medical records I reviewed over forty years—your documented journeys, though I never met most of you, shaped my understanding of how bodies respond to trauma and sometimes find ways forward.

To the therapists and healers who admitted when they didn't have answers, who acknowledged that healing isn't linear, who said "I don't know" when they didn't know. Your honesty was more valuable than false certainty.

To the researchers whose work I've attempted to understand and translate: Vincent Felitti, Bessel van der Kolk, Stephen Porges, Peter Levine, Daniel Siegel, and many others. This book integrates peer-reviewed research with clinical observations and lived experience. While I've strived for accuracy in representing scientific findings, the science of trauma and nervous system regulation continues to evolve. Any errors in interpretation are mine alone.

To those who trusted me with their nervous system journeys and taught me that everyone's path looks different. Your willingness to experiment with these approaches—and your honest feedback when things didn't help—shaped every page.

> To everyone who checks locks five times, leaves their body during conversations, or says yes when they mean no:
>
> You're not broken. You never were.
>
> Your patterns make sense. They protected you once. Some still do.
>
> This book is for you, from someone still checking her own locks, still noticing her patterns, still practicing awareness one moment at a time.

Note on Privacy: *Names and identifying details have been changed throughout this book to protect privacy. The stories are composites drawn from multiple experiences, arranged to illustrate specific patterns and healing processes. Any resemblance to specific individuals is coincidental.*

A Personal Request

If this book helped you understand your patterns, notice your nervous system, or feel less alone in your struggles, would you consider leaving a review?

Reviews help other people find this book—people who are checking locks at 3 AM, floating near ceilings during conversations, or wondering why they can't just "get over it."

Even a brief review mentioning one thing that resonated makes a difference. You don't need to share personal details— just whether the book helped.

Your review might be the reason someone else finds the understanding they need.

Thank you for reading, for noticing, for practicing awareness.

The work continues, breath by breath, moment by moment.

— With ongoing practice and gratitude

www.ingramcontent.com/pod-product-compliance
Lightning Source LLC
Chambersburg PA
CBHW051608120626
46551CB00014B/1715